CAREER RENEGADE

CAREER
RENEGADE

How to Make a Great Living
Doing What You Love

Jonathan Fields

BROADWAY BOOKS

New York

BROADWAY

Published in the United States by Broadway Books,
an imprint of The Doubleday Publishing Group,
a division of Random House, Inc., New York.
www.broadwaybooks.com

BROADWAY BOOKS and its logo, a letter B bisected on the
diagonal, are trademarks of Random House, Inc.

Book design by Nicola Ferguson

Library of Congress Cataloging-in-Publication Data

Fields, Jonathan.
    Career renegade : how to make a great living doing what
you love / Jonathan Fields. — 1st ed.
        p. cm.
    1. Success in business.   2. Career development.   I. Title.

HF5386.F4145 2008
650.14—dc22
2008021986

ISBN 978-0-7679-2741-3

PRINTED IN THE UNITED STATES OF AMERICA

10 9 8 7 6 5 4 3 2 1

First Edition

To Stephanie and Jesse, my rock
and my inspiration

Your work is going to fill a large part of your life, and the only way to be truly satisfied is to do what you believe is great work. And the only way to do great work is to love what you do.

—STEVE JOBS, *2005 Stanford Commencement*

Contents

CONTENTS

Acknowledgments

Crafting this book took equal parts of blood, sweat, tears, laughter, and even a little Hell's Kitchen pixie dust! My driving purpose was to deliver something that was not only fun and inspirational, but insanely useful. No easy task. To those who were instrumental in making it what it is today, I am deeply grateful.

My wife, Stephanie, and daughter, Jesse, are just plain amazing. They've endured not only the writing of this book, but the professional journey that served as its backdrop. Many nights were spent snuggled on the couch with my notebook in my lap and my little girl drifting to sleep against my side. You guys rock!

My fabulous family gave me the sense of self needed to take risks, to discover what I really wanted to be when I grow up, the confidence to write about it, and the discretion to know where to draw the line.

My editor, Becky Cole, not only got who I was (a herculean achievement), but understood what this book needed to become long before I saw it, then gave me precious latitude with my ideas and voice.

Wendy Sherman, my agent, believed I had something to offer and has been an enduring source of guidance, confidence, and friendship.

My friends, now you know what I've been up to for the last few years, thanks for hanging in there. My schedule just opened up, let's do lunch.

All the amazing people who were gracious enough to share their stories, insights, ideas, many who appear in this book and some who, because of editorial and space limitations, do not, a huge thanks.

Shelley Adelle, my studio-manager, research assistant, and doer of any and everything that helps make my life easier and better, thanks for your smiling energy.

And, to all of my students, teachers, and fellow career renegades, the journey's just begun.

CAREER RENEGADE

Introduction

IT'S FUNNY HOW THE CORPORATE grind gets hold of you.

By the time you graduate college or grad school, a mountain of debt keeps you locked into a quest to earn as much as possible and pay off your loans. With each year, you earn more and fight your way up the ladder. But, then, an odd thing happens.

You don't ever get free.

At some point, it dawns on you that the corporate ladder is really more of a treadmill. You run faster, work harder, climb higher, sweat more blood, and push through stifling fatigue. But, in the end, all too often, you're no freer or happier than the day you began. In fact, for many, as your lifestyle expands to gobble up nearly every dollar you make, it's quite the opposite.

The day-to-day stress, relentless posturing, politics, negotiating, and hours spent on minutiae increasingly suck the life out of you. Body, mind, and spirit, slowly and methodically being sucked dry.

Maybe it would be more tolerable if you actually cared about what you did, if you earned your living doing something you truly loved. But, like millions of others, you're likely less than inspired by the culture and content of the one thing that consumes half of your waking hours. You've got that "same job, different day" itch, where personal fulfillment, passion, and mission have long ago taken a backseat to the mad dash for cash.

And, you begin to wonder if there's a different way.

What if you could actually do what you love for a living without leaving your life behind? What if that mad passion that everyone says can't make money, done differently, could allow you to make a great living? What if no matter how entrenched you are in the life you're leading, it was possible, very possible, to extract yourself from a misery-drenched, life-sucking job and grow a future defined not by your ability to endure suffering, but by taking the opportunity to love what you do, enjoy life today, and create an equally secure tomorrow?

What if you could really pull this off without blowing apart everything you've worked so hard to create?

Would you want in?

Yes?

Then, here's something you should know . . .

It's entirely possible.

How do I know? Because, I've done it. I went from six figure, Law Review, SEC, mega-firm Manhattan attorney to serial lifestyle entrepreneur, speaker, writer, marketing gun, yoga innovator, artist, and author. Along the way, I've made a lot of great calls and a lot of big, fat, stupid mistakes that I like to call "learning experiences."

I've built a string of health and fitness companies that have changed the lives of tens of thousands of people, helped create multimillion-dollar brands, written articles and stories and contributed to books and national magazines, trained CEOs, taught yoga to movie stars, cultivated a nice six-figure living, and carved out time to be with my wife and pick up my daughter from school.

I've created business innovations that led to appearances in the *New York Times,* the *Wall Street Journal, Entrepreneur .com, MSNBC, SmartMoneyTV, Forbes.com, Fine Living,* the *New York Post,* the *Daily News, Vogue, Elle, Self, Fitness, Outside, More,* and thousands of other publications, websites, and blogs.

Why do you care? Because, not too long ago, I was you.

And the single greatest thing that stopped me from doing what I loved was the fear that I'd either end up poor or a failure—or both. What a load of life-stifling crap.

My Wake-up Call

It's been a dozen years since I made the jump. I began as an enforcement attorney at the U.S. Securities and Exchange Commission in New York, then jumped to a top New York law firm as a securities/hedge-fund lawyer, before my body literally rejected my career.

I'd been working nearly seventy-two hours straight, each one more excruciating than the one before. But, missing the deadline meant losing $100 million for our client, so I pressed on until we finally closed the deal. I staggered into a cab, passed out for a few hours, then headed straight to my doctor's office.

His face turned ghostly white as he grabbed my hand, whisked me through a team of specialists, and sent me straight to the hospital for emergency surgery.

Weeks of relentless hours had literally collapsed my immune system, allowing a softball-sized infection to ravage my intestines and eat a whole through them from the outside in. Within hours, I was in the OR. Thankfully, I made it through, battered, but on the way to a full recovery. I had plenty of time to sit around and think while I was healing. Talk about a wake-up call!

I needed to find another way. There had to be something more.

Two weeks later, I sat in my office desperately scribbling on a legal pad with a mile-wide smile on my face. I couldn't write fast enough.

What spilled forth was not legal jargon but rather a quickly growing list of things I thought would be insanely cool to do for a living—activities that, at various points in my life, I had developed a deep interest in or mad passion for but relegated to the level of hobby because everyone else told me I'd never make money doing them.

Nonsense!

I wondered what would happen if I turned the work ethic and innovation that landed me at one of the most elite law firms in the world loose on the quest to figure out how to transform my interests and passions into enough money to live well in the world?

With that, an odyssey was born. My goal was three-fold:

- Make a great living
- Love what I did
- Be around people I loved

And so I started out on a new path.

It took a massive investment of both time and energy. And, a willingness to do a lot of things right, spend a lot of money testing different ideas, and, admittedly, do a bunch of things wrong.

Over a period of years, I began to discover certain processes, steps, resources, and actions that could transform nearly any passion into a wellspring of money.

Building on this knowledge, I turned:

- A passion for health and fitness into one of the most successful personal-training facilities in the country
- A lifelong interest in the mind-body connection into a top-grossing yoga center and teacher-training institute
- A love of writing into a career as an author, magazine contributor, and blogger
- A zest for learning and the psychology of persuasion into a boutique direct-marketing group
- A love of teaching and entrepreneurship into my career renegade training company
- A mad passion to love what I do and spend as much time as possible playing with my family into a serious living built around the lifestyle I hold dear

Sounds Great, but Will the Money *Really* Follow?

For the last few years, wherever I go, people want to discover how to become a career renegade. They all want to know how to turn something, whether it's knitting, painting, writing, or growing grapes, into enough cash to call it a living. Especially when everyone around them keeps telling them it's just not possible.

The conversation inevitably turns to the two giant questions that stop nearly everyone in their tracks:

1. What if the thing that makes my heart sing doesn't pay enough to support me?
2. Or, what if it could be lucrative, but only if I was at the top of the field?

For most people, this is where the conversation ends. Because there are no easy answers. I am not a big believer in the old "do what you love and either the money will follow or you'll be so damn happy it won't matter anymore" school of thought.

I live in New York City. I have a family to support. I need to earn six figures just to scrape by. I've had to work incredibly hard and think wildly outside of the box (hell, half the time I've had to create my own box to think outside of) to find ways to make the money follow.

And, that, my friends, is what this book is all about.

This is not a career guide like any other.

The focus here is quite different, because this book answers the question everyone else avoids: What about the money? I've read a lot of books, been to a lot of seminars, spent thousands of dollars, and all too often walked away annoyed and let down. And I swore if I ever decided to reveal the tools, techniques, and resources I'd accumulated, it would be the real deal.

So, here's a short list of what this book is not . . .

- You will not be forced to endure pages of fluffy, feel-good mumbo jumbo, life's too short.
- You will not be dragged through the litany of steps needed to explore, select, and find another career that will leave you financially improved, but still scratching your head wondering when you can quit and finally do something with your life.
- You will not be given a partial solution and then pitched the chance to pay thousands more for the remaining 25 percent of the puzzle.
- You will not be given advice from someone who's only studied how to succeed, but never succeeded at anything other than telling you what to do.
- You will not be given the ridiculous instructions to

abandon everyone who disagrees with you or stops you from doing what's in your heart.

- You will not simply be told stories that leave you inspired, but are devoid of specific, actionable tips, tools, and techniques.

The simple truth is you can turn nearly any passion into a big, fat heap of money. However, it often requires mining aspects of those passions you never knew existed or bringing them to life in markets and ways that defy the mainstream.

With nearly every move I've made, there's been an army waiting to tell me, "You can't do that!" In the beginning, I'd try to argue. Now, I tell them, "Just watch me," and go ahead and do that very thing they've convinced themselves is undoable.

I've also had the incredible fortune to meet and befriend a growing cadre of like-minded career renegades over the years, people who have enjoyed similar journeys and succeeded in myriad pursuits, often creating new professional paradigms along the way.

In the pages that follow, you'll meet a married father of six who left a nearly twenty-year career as a reporter to earn even more money blogging about lifestyles and simplicity. You'll find an office worker who turned a buried passion for art into a great living painting vineyards in Napa and a visual artist who found an outlet and a serious income in the world of baking. You'll revel along with an orthopedic surgeon who turned a passion for growing coffee in Kona, Hawaii, into a lucrative second career and explore how a technology sales executive became a personal-development pundit. These are just a few of the many case studies that will guide your journey.

This book reveals the fundamental principals, strategies, tools, and techniques that have fueled our collective adventures and inspired not only success, but boundless passion and, for some, extraordinary wealth.

In the pages that follow, you will discover:

- How to find out if your passion really can generate a nice living.
- How to mine, redeploy, exploit, monetize, leverage, commoditize, and repurpose your seemingly money-less passion to make it generate the income you need.
- How to test your passion for market demand and adapt or modify it to bring it to life in the most lucrative way possible.
- How to build your knowledge, skills, and abilities to a level of mastery quickly and inexpensively.
- How to build on your mastery to establish yourself as

a known expert and leverage your authority to create economic opportunity.

- How to master fear of failure, program your mind for success, and cultivate the renegade mind-set.
- How to convince those you love you're not insane and make them enthusiastic about your career renegade journey.
- How to build your renegade career on the side, until it's established enough for you to decide whether to jump into it full time.
- How to tap a giant collection of career renegade tools, techniques, technologies, resources, and websites that will dramatically accelerate your quest.

Sound like a big promise? It is. Life's too short for small ones. Welcome to the ranks of the Career Renegade.

PART 1

*What Makes You
Come Alive?*

ONE

You Don't Have to Be World Class to Make a World-Class Living

MUCH TO THE CONTRARY OF what we've been told for the better part of our lives, we do not exist for the sole purpose of paying our bills, grooming our kids to be able to do the same, and maybe, someday, retiring to finally enjoy life, should we ever reach that point.

We are here to let our lights shine as brightly as possible, to drink in the joy of friendship and family, to serve and better the greater community, and to tap into and inspire passion in everything we do. We are here to come alive. In doing so, we serve as an example to others that a life beyond muddling by is not only possible, but mandatory.

But, we've got a problem. We've spent years or decades

believing the thing or things we love to do could never generate enough money to rise above the level of a hobby. We've bought into the notion that the ability to cash in on your passion is a wayward dream for gifted athletes, movie stars, and legends in their fields, people who are world-class great. And, as much as we might love to paint, act, play games, or run marathons, we're never playing pro ball, fronting a gallery show at Bogosian, or opening for Bruce at the Garden.

This might surprise you, but, for the most part, I agree.

You will probably never become world class. Especially if you are already deeply entrenched in a life and lifestyle that would not easily support the years or decades of hyperfocused deliberate practice needed to attain elite status. Or, if you have unchangeable limitations that stand between you and greatness. At five foot nine and forty-two years old, I am never playing center for the Knicks.

But, here's the big news, you don't have to be world-class great to make a great living doing what you love if you are willing to step outside the box, approach your passion differently, find innovative ways to mine that passion for money, and work like crazy to make it happen.

Running from the Law

In the last few months before I left the law, I began to rekindle my passion for the study of the human body and its connection to movement and mind-set. As a lawyer, I had explored yoga as a means of stress management, but I was nowhere near accomplished enough to teach it. So, I turned to fitness, drawing upon over a decade of year-round training in gymnastics, while reading everything I could find on anatomy and kinesiology.

I earned the first of many fitness certifications while still practicing law, resigned a few weeks later, and talked my way into a personal training position in an exclusive fitness studio on Manhattan's Upper East Side. I got to wear sneakers and hang out running in the park all day while learning this new trade. I knew my nest egg from the law would carry me for about a year.

The first few months were an eye-opener. I learned that most personal trainers made very little money and often left the field or worked other jobs to fill in the gaps. It was rare that a trainer would earn enough to pay the rent for a studio apartment, let alone support a family in New York.

Where There's a Will, There's a Payday

I also found, though, that a handful of people were able to define and differentiate themselves in a way that made them more successful with clients, gave them more satisfaction in their careers, and generated significant six-figure incomes.

I began to believe I could create a better lifestyle mouse-trap. And, even though I was confident I'd never be part of the elite trainer set, I knew I could create a personal fitness solution that would generate substantially more money than most.

After about six months learning the business hands-on as a trainer and researching the industry, I left to build a private practice, while I laid the groundwork to launch a new facility. I wanted to create an environment where people could feel immediately comfortable, even if they'd never exercised. Images of a friendly southwestern retreat came to mind.

Of course, it wasn't long before much more experienced colleagues in the fitness industry began to ask, "Who do you think you are to open a fitness facility after only months in the business? You can't do that."

In fall 1997, I launched Sedona Private Fitness in Cedar Grove, New Jersey, along with a more experienced fitness partner to lend credibility and bring start-up clientele. By creating an atmosphere that was intentionally homey and developing a brand that held appeal to educated, affluent adults who wanted to get healthy but hated gyms, Sedona was a smash hit. It was super-accessible, luxurious, and results-oriented. While small in size, Sedona generated almost as much training revenue in one month as the average full-size health club earned in a year.

So Much for Conventional Wisdom

A few years in, change was in the air. Along with the growth of Sedona over the next few years, my lifestyle interests and commitments began to evolve. I was married, living in Manhattan, working in New Jersey and, while I enjoyed what I did, I really wanted to be back in the city. Plus, with Sedona humming and the hypercreative element of the business cycle coming to a close, I began to hunger for a new challenge.

I decided to sell my interest in Sedona to private investors and refocus my energies. On the heels of the sale, I was pretty confident in my ability to succeed, so I took some time off, did a lot of writing, and began to cultivate my interest in broader mind-body lifestyles, with a focus on yoga and wellness.

As my personal yoga practice developed and my focus returned to New York, my mind began, once again, to spin. This is fun, this is cool, this makes me feel good. Then the questions began. Can I build on this new mind-body/yoga passion in a way that would differentiate what I do from what everyone else does? If so, does the world really need it? And, of course, can I make a living at it and, if I can't, will my wife leave me?

I immersed myself more deeply in the study of yoga, while exploring its potential for generating a comfortable living. At that point, my wife was pregnant and, while I was still led by passion, I needed to convince myself that the next adventure held the economic potential to comfortably support a family in New York City. That's a tall order for a recovering lawyer, let alone a yogi.

I learned that while yoga practice was expansive and powerful, earning a living as a teacher was a rarity. Once again, conventional wisdom said don't bother. Indeed, in India, for much of the yogic tradition, teachers were ascetics and beggars, who subsisted on the generosity of others. Only in the last twenty years has yoga emerged as a more mainstream professional pursuit in its own country of origin. Still, I saw the power of the practice, the size of the untapped market, and, more importantly, a specific segment that was being overlooked. This was the opening I had been searching for.

On September 10, 2001, I signed the lease for what would become Sonic Yoga NYC, the first major Manhattan studio with an emphasis on preserving the power of yoga, while reducing barriers to participation for regular, decidedly unfoofy grown-ups.

In the seven years since its launch, Sonic Yoga has grown to become the number-one-rated center in New York City (Citysearch 2005–2008) and boasts one of the busiest teacher training schools in the Northeast.

Was I the best trainer or yoga teacher? Nope. But, I immersed myself in both fields, blended my experience in the fitness and lifestyle world with my background in business, and achieved a level of accomplishment that allowed me to be well paid.

And, as my interests and passions continued to expand to writing, direct marketing, speaking, and entrepreneurship training, I've been able to structure my yoga studio to contribute very nicely to my income mix, while taking only five to ten hours a week of my time. Sounds nice, doesn't it?

Now, let's figure out how to turn your passion into a career, renegade style.

TWO

What's Your Secret Passion?

ASK AN EIGHT-YEAR-OLD what he loves to do and you'll get answers like play baseball or basketball, dance, play chess or video games, dress up dolls, paint, cook, build Lego houses, or design chocolate lollipops.

Kids have this ability to tap into what jazzes them in a way that adults find impossible. Sometimes it's one thing, sometimes many. They don't struggle with what they want to do. They just acknowledge what they "love" to do and believe "if I love it and I can do it all I want *now*, why can't I keep doing it *when I grow up*? Why can't it be my job?"

Good question. Why can't it?

The short answer is—it can. But you may need to go

about it in a way that defies the mainstream. The better part of this book is devoted to that process. Before we get there, though, we need to get reacquainted with exactly what it is that makes you come alive.

I have two questions for you:

- What activity would you do for free, purely out of a sense of passion?
- Imagine you woke up this morning to a phone call saying you had just won the state lottery. It was all yours, but there was a condition: You had to continue to work for the rest of your life and you could use the money to live on, but not to fund any professional endeavor. Now, what would you do? Write it down.

Chances are one or more answers jumped out, followed almost immediately by that little voice that said, "But, I could never actually make money doing that, so why bother?" This entire book will answer that question. It will reveal renegade paths designed to bring your passion to life in a way that generates real money.

So, go ahead and make your list. Write down the activities that make you come alive, the ones you'd love to call your living if you believed they'd truly support you. Maybe it's one thing, maybe it's dozens. Either way, just do it.

This list is a great starting place; it allows you to embark upon the next leg of your career journey with meaning and joy. But there are two more elements we want to work into the mix. Including them, regardless of the activity you choose, will go a long way toward ensuring that you not only do something meaningful and lucrative, but you do it in a way and with people that'll make each day a joy.

Those turbocharging elements are flow and people.

The Power of Flow

I was about eleven or twelve years old when I began to paint. I stole a small corner of my mom's basement pottery workshop as my own and began to experiment with an old set of oil paints my grandmother had given me. I had no training, but the challenge of understanding and working with this complex medium fascinated me. I set an old door on top of a few fifty-pound boxes of clay, hooked up an architect's swing-arm lamp, and began to play. I found myself spending longer and longer in my little corner studio, often with the entire rest of the workshop in darkness as I worked under the light of the swing-arm lamp.

As I became more comfortable painting, the process of creation took hold and, with no daylight to tell me what time it was, I would literally lose days to my little corner of the basement, utterly consumed by my exploration. It was through this process that I began to understand the reach and impact of the extraordinary state of absorption that my mother would regularly escape into while throwing pots.

Over the years, I have been able to cultivate that same absorbed state through a number of different activities. As a competitive gymnast in high school, the moment my fingers touched the high bar, the world around me ceased to exist. In a windowless, college computer lab, deep in the creation of a program, day turned to night and back to day in the blink of an eye. Mountain biking quickly through winding, rugged trails buried deep in the woods or climbing the craggy faces of local mountains delivered me into a state where past and future ceased to exist. Writing takes me there, too: A place where I am fully engaged in the world, in the moment, yet completely and utterly immersed in what athletes and artists have come to call "the zone."

It was decades after I first felt the thrill of being so absorbed that I heard this highly absorbed state described by famed cognitive psychologist Mihály Csikszentmihályi (pronounced "cheeks-sent-me-high") as "flow" and learned of its elements and critical importance in finding satisfaction in both work and life.

According to Csikszentmihályi, while the state of flow may occur across a wide spectrum of activities and be experienced differently by each person, there are certain shared elements that most often define this rapturous state. These include:

Working toward a clear goal with a well-defined process: The task, big or small, must be clearly defined and the steps needed to get there must be laid out in detail or at least be highly delineated along the way. Getting there does not have to be easy, but you need to be able to see, even from a distance, where you are going.

Cultivating deep concentration: The nature of the job must require an intense sense of concentration. Examples would be a fast-moving game like Ping-Pong or a gymnastics routine. In a work setting, leading a high-stakes, face-to-face negotiation, drafting a document, writing a blog post, creating a detailed artistic rendering, or coding a computer game, animation, or program would qualify.

Lack of a sense of self-consciousness: You become so engaged in the nature of the work that you are no longer aware of yourself but rather feel a sense of total absorption in the task. It's like that old sports adage, "be the ball."

Altered sense of time: Time seems to either stand still or fly by in the blink of an eye.

Ongoing, direct feedback: Either through people or the testable nature of the task, you need regular enough feedback to be able to constantly adapt, correct course, and make progress toward your goal. For example, when writing a computer program, you can constantly test, and debug to ensure you are on the right track.

Task is highly challenging, but doable: The task must be hard enough to finish that it requires a significant investment of your attention, resources, and energy, leading to the sense of absorption. But, it also has to be easy enough to allow you to believe that a solution is, in fact, possible, or else you'd just give up.

Control over the means: You must have the ability to harness the resources to get the job done. Lack of control over the means to achieve a goal, whether it's been set by you or demanded of you, is actually the source of a huge amount of job stress. Let's say, for example, you were charged with painting a house in a week but were required to use only organic paint. If you had the ability to manufacture organic paint, you would not need to rely on anyone else to complete this very challenging task. Everything you needed to get the job done would be within your control. If, however, you needed to purchase the paint from an organic paint manufacturer, and they were backed up that week, you would have to rely on someone else to contribute a critical factor to the process. And, if they were backed up, you would be stuck in limbo, waiting for them to do their part. This would take you out of flow.

The activity is meaningful or intrinsically rewarding by the very nature of doing it: While the end result might entitle you to a big outside reward, like a bonus, raise, or high sale price, the essential nature of the activity is so rewarding that you would do it at the same level, even without the extra motivation of some kind of external prize. For example, most great artists don't paint for a paycheck, they paint because the very process of painting is so woven into who they are that not painting would be akin to not breathing.

While not every element need be present to effect a state of flow, the greater the number of elements, the deeper into a state of flow you will be delivered.

Csikszentmihályi's decades of research speak to the life-enhancing impact of exploring ways to increasingly incorporate flow into all aspects of life. So, when you look at your list of things you'd love to do for a living, ask yourself which pursuits most often deliver you into a state of flow. As you plot your renegade path, keep those activities in the forefront of your mind.

Flow is a great experience enhancer. But, equally important to our enjoyment of any pursuit are the people around us.

The Power of People

Barring the rare happy hermit, Csikszentmihályi also reveals that most of us thrive to a greater extent when we are around others, especially like-minded others. Yes, even stressed-out, solitude-seeking people. Human beings are innately social. But, *who* we are social with determines to a large extent how satisfied we are with what we are doing at any given point.

When I speak I am often asked about the benefits of being a bit of an entrepreneur. People say, "It must be amazing to have total control over your life, to work when you want to, to make as much as you want, to have control over every aspect of your job." We'll get to how much of fact and fantasy there is in that statement later, but people are universally surprised when I answer, "Actually, the best part of being an entrepreneur is *not* the control you gain over wealth, but the chance to handpick the people you surround yourself with and create an organizational culture that is completely in sync with who you are." Translation, it's all about the Benjamins, not the benjamins.

The way you relate to those around you, and they to you, can not only color, but, in large part, define your experience of work and life.

If you take an identical job, setting, and paycheck and swap in a different set of players, your title may remain unchanged, but your experience of that same job becomes radically different. Indeed, an April 2007 study from U.K. consulting firm, Chiumento, revealed 73 percent of employees said good relationships with colleagues were the key source of job enjoyment, while only 48 percent pointed to money.

This would come as no surprise to *Vital Friends* author and Gallup Organization Workplace Research and Leadership Consulting head, Tom Rath. In his fascinating exploration of friendship both in and out of the workplace, he discovered:

- People with a best friend at work are seven-times more likely to be engaged in their work.
- Close friendships at work boost employee satisfaction by nearly 50 percent.
- People with at least three close friends at work were 46 percent more likely to be extremely satisfied with their job and 88 percent more likely to be satisfied with their lives.
- Being around a boss was generally considered the

least pleasant part of the workday. But, employees who are good friends with their bosses are more than twice as likely to be happy with their work.

So, when I finally had the chance to choose whom I would work with, I was in heaven. That doesn't mean I always chose right, but at least I chose. And, as you might have guessed, while I take my work very seriously, I also like to enjoy myself and make sure others are having fun along the way.

Over the last ten years, no matter how much stress the business of being a multitentacled entrepreneur has created, there has never been a day where I've woken up wishing I didn't have to go to work.

But, what if you're not an entrepreneur? What if you don't have the ability to create the culture or hire your colleagues? What if your dream career just happens to exist in a place where the culture and the people have already been chosen and created—and those people are not the people you want to spend the majority of your waking life with?

Two options: Grin and bear it and hope to rise into a position of authority quickly enough to influence the evolution of your organization's culture and people, or choose to join or create a different setting where you either immediately mesh with those around you on a much deeper level or have the ability to contribute significantly to the hiring and culture more quickly.

There is no such thing as a dream job with a nightmare culture or staff. It's a package deal.

Bringing Together Experience, Flow, and People

Time to bring it all together and integrate experience, flow, and people. On a piece of paper, write the following:

- Lifelong Jones. What are the activities or pursuits that you'd love to do as a living for the rest of your life if you believed they could earn you enough to live comfortably in the world?
- Flow Generators. Which activities on this list have led you into flow states? If none have, it's probably a sign that you need to dig deeper to find activities and pursuits that offer at least passing opportunities for flow.
- People Power. What types of people and culture do you feel most alive around?

Now, start with the item on your Lifelong Jones list that's calling you the strongest and is most likely to integrate the elements of flow and surround you with the type of people you love to be around. Let's see how we can turn that into a serious living.

PART 2

*What Kind of Renegade
Will You Be?*

THREE

Introducing the Career Renegade Paths

FOR THE CAREER RENEGADE, conventional wisdom is actually a great asset. It thins the herd of competitors, leaving only those who choose to blaze their own path, rather than follow another's. It creates space for those who lead with passion to truly shine.

Your first challenge is to understand this, to see conventional wisdom as simply the first of many tests, the collective presumptions of other people who have not been able to succeed in their own quests. Or, even more likely, a reflection of an unwillingness to ever try. Know this, accept it. Then resolve to move beyond it.

Moving Beyond the Mainstream

This chapter will introduce you to a number of renegade paths, approaches to turning something that should, by all rights, make you happy but poor into something that puts a smile on your face and money in your bank account. Following these paths may make you a bit nervous. But, as Kierkegaard said, "Anxiety is the dizziness of freedom."

As the book unfolds, you'll also meet many people who've succeeded at what you strive to achieve. And, you'll find a set of tools that will keep you maximally supported, help minimize your risk, build your knowledge and reputation and guide you through a gradual process of evolution.

While the paths to transforming a moneyless passion into a lucrative future are limited only by your own creativity, we'll focus in on seven proven career renegade paths:

- Redeploying your passion in a hungrier market (chapter 4)
- Refocusing and mining the most lucrative micro-markets (chapter 4)
- Exploiting gaps in the information needed to excel at an activity (chapter 5)
- Exploiting gaps in education (chapter 6)
- Exploiting gaps in gear or merchandise (chapter 7)
- Exploiting gaps in community (chapter 8)

- Exploiting gaps in the way a pursuit is provided (chapter 9)

The first and second paths are about discovering opportunities in alternative markets or highly specialized niche markets. The next five paths fall under the umbrella of something called *exploits*. Exploits are career or entrepreneurial opportunities that exist due to a need that is not being fully satisfied. Exploits are often the source of tremendous economic reward.

There are many ways to pursue your passion in a way that is financially rewarding. For some people, the above career renegade paths will serve as precise templates for success. For others, they'll act more as guidelines to be adapted. Don't be surprised if your journey blends aspects of a number of paths. Because, once you begin to remove the blinders of conventional wisdom, you'll begin to discover options that may have been sitting in front of your nose for years.

FOUR

Turn Your Passion Loose in Unexpected Places

IT'S TIME TO START DOWN the road less traveled. If the pursuit that makes you come alive won't easily pay the bills, explore bringing your passion to life in alternative or niche markets that value it on a whole different level.

Redeploy Your Passion in a Market That Places a Higher Value on It

In the world of fine arts, Liv Hansen was just another faceless artist trying to beg, borrow, or steal her way into a limelight that tens of thousands of others strove toward. Sure, she had talent, but she was competing in a market populated by thousands of people with similar talent vying for a handful of openings. Standing out in that market was a near impossibility.

But, what happens when you take that same all-consuming passion to create, formal artistic training, and ability and turn it loose on a radically different market? One that strongly values artistry, but is defined largely by production? One that allows hypercreative abilities to strongly differentiate a product and serves a massive consumer base at a price point that makes these creations accessible to nearly everyone?

I'll tell you what happens. You create opportunity out of thin air.

Liv's Story

How to Get People to Stand in Line to Eat Your Art

Graduating with a bachelor of fine arts from Cornell in 1992, Liv Hansen was stumped. She'd followed her consuming passion for visual creativity into a degree that was, well, less than marketable. Now, school was out and it was time to make a living.

So, Liv did what most BFA grads did. She returned to her hometown in Nyack, New York, and began knocking on local art-world doors, while suffering through a string of odd jobs to pay the rent. Her mixed-media creations landed in a few local group shows, but, after two years of hustling, bigger doors never opened. Struggling with her own self-doubt, she gradually relented to the notion that her art was "something I'll just have to do on the side."

Right around this time, Liv's mom, Kaye, bought a little bakery just across the Hudson in Ardsley, New York. The Riviera Bakehouse was a mom and pop business that had been around for years. As Liv's mom and stepdad prepared to take over the running of the bakery, Kaye asked Liv if she wanted to help out and make some extra cash.

Her parents had owned a bakery when Liv was younger, so she knew her way around the kitchen and front counter and had iced more than her share of cupcakes. And, like so many other kids who grew up helping out in the family business, she swore she'd never go back into it. The food business, she knew, could be brutal. The hours were terrible, stress was high, and working conditions were often cramped, stressful, and hot.

But, with her bank account hovering on low and the chance to "get back on her feet," she took her mom's offer. Besides, she loved being with her mother and she knew the business. Still, in her mind, this was just a stopgap until her real job came along.

She began working the counter and decorating cupcakes, but, before long her cupcakes began to take on a new role. They weren't just treats to be iced and put out for sale. They were mini-canvases upon which she might let her wild imagination run free. Wedding cakes became opportunities to mesmerize and kids birthday cakes turned into storyboards. Through this process something very unexpected began to happen, she was actually starting to have fun.

Fueled by the opportunity to take her edible canvases to a whole new level, Liv began to use melted chocolate to literally paint the scenes in her imagination. Out came wild animals, vivid floral explosions, and Litchtensteinesque comics. The opportunities were endless.

Liv's creations were creating such a buzz that people started coming from other towns to take a gander at her edible art and then savor the objects of their envy, not just with their eyes, but their noses, mouths, and bellies.

Soon after, Liv and her mom decided to take a big step. They moved the bakery to its own building, nearly four times the size of the old bakery. Over the years, the growing notoriety of the Riviera Bakehouse has spawned a series of hugely popular books and television appearances.

Now, married with a family, Liv works more as the visionary, the artistic director, and lets her family of bakers bring her creations to life. This gave her space to be a mom, a daughter, and an artist.

The key to Liv's success in transforming a job with little apparent connection to her passion lay in her ability to see a potential market for her creative juices that stepped beyond the confines of what most would consider a viable medium for "art."

Simply put, she figured out a way to redeploy her passion into, forgive me, a far hungrier market.

Refocus and Mine the Most Lucrative Submarkets

Liv ended up cashing in on her artistic passion in a completely unrelated, yet far hungrier market. Artist Ann Rea took a different route. Rather than finding opportunity by applying her passion to a new market, she found her opening by drastically narrowing the existing market.

Ann's Story
Office Worker Finds Artistic Opportunity in Wine Country

Coming off seven years in a variety of increasingly draining office jobs, Ann Rea was burned-out and propped up on antidepressants. She knew she had to make a change, to get out of the environment she was in, but she wasn't sure what to do. She had a degree in fine arts, but hadn't picked up a paintbrush in nearly seven years. Plus, conventional wisdom said nobody makes a living as an artist without being famous.

Around that time, she met acclaimed artist Wayne Thiebaud, who told her she needed to quit her job and start painting. But Ann wasn't about to give up the comfortable lifestyle she'd built. So she began to brainstorm, creating a list of every conceivable way she could earn money as an artist. She was determined to find an answer.

Living in northern California, Ann was acquainted with the incredible vistas, vineyards, and culture of Napa Valley's wine country. And, as she made out her list, she began to explore the intersection between the wine culture and the art-buying community. It didn't take long for the lightbulb to pop on.

What if she partnered with the wineries to paint pictures of their vineyards, then used the tasting rooms as galleries to sell the finished works of art? The vineyards would capture additional revenue and visitors would get to take home a beautiful reminder of the vineyard and boast the possession of a new work of art. And, once home and displayed on collectors' walls, the paintings would serve not only as works of art, but advertisements for both Ann and the vineyards she painted. It seemed a perfect market to move into.

Ann began to approach wineries in Napa and Sonoma, one at a time, with her idea and the combination of her talent, the beautiful setting, and the relaxed, wine-infused atmosphere worked its magic. Her work immediately caught fire, leading to private commissions and large-scale commercial work.

Not content with this level of success, Ann continued to explore ways to make money from her work. She began reading every book she could find on business formats, intellectual property, and marketing and eventually decided to create a combination of high-end full-sized giclée prints for display, notecards, wedding invitations, and even labels for wine bottles. And, to support her effort, she launched an online gallery and store at www.AnnRea.com.

Ann's story is a great example of finding a very lucrative, specialized micro-niche in the field of your passion and serving that niche in a way that creates a great living. Ann's story doesn't end there though.

It turns out, Ann was not the only artist with a strong desire to make a nice living. As word spread about Ann and her unique approach to marketing and selling art, other artists began asking her to share her insights. And, as more people asked, Ann tapped her now deep reservoir of business and marketing skills to begin coaching artists and leading marketing seminars for artists. Put another way, she leveraged her unique knowledge to create a second business opportunity by providing information, by teaching others how to do what she'd done. She exploited an education gap. We'll explore this path in detail in the next few chapters.

In this way, Ann is a great example of how one career renegade path often leads to a second opportunity in sharing how you've accomplished something that others would kill to accomplish.

What Are the Key Elements of a Good Market to Redeploy Your Passion?

In thinking about potential alternative markets or trying to find smaller, more lucrative submarkets, think about fields, careers, jobs, or paths where the elements of what you love to do are valued, but in short supply. You are looking for a market where your passion leads to:

Differentiation: Does what you love to do or create strongly differentiate you from most everyone else and add substantial value over and above the normal expectations of consumers in that market? While Liv's artistic ability was not a huge differentiator in the sea of others in the mainstream art world, it was a huge differentiator in the world of cakes. When I left the law to start out as a personal trainer, my ability to talk intelligently about the world of venture capital, hedge funds, and mergers and acquisitions differentiated me from nearly every other trainer and was a serious asset in attracting clients who made their livings in the world I'd recently left.

Hunger: Will people want what you are offering? Even if being a master of your passion would make you different, would redeploying your passion into this new market create a product or service that would make large numbers of people trip over each other to get? Even if Liv's talent let her create magical, radically different cakes, if there was no strong demand for such whimsical designs, it wouldn't have mattered. The fact that cakes are designed not only to be eaten, but to impress, made people hunger for Liv's high-

profile creations. Similarly, Ann's field studies and repro-
ductions, while beautiful, were offered in a manner and in
a highly unique environment that was far more conducive
to buying. Ann gave people exactly what they wanted in the
place and at the time they were most likely to buy.

Price availability: Can you deliver a product or service into this new market at a price point that generates
substantial demand? This does not necessarily mean it has
to be cheap, just at a price point where there is a sizable,
constantly renewable group of people ready and willing to
spend money on what you have to offer. Ann realized that,
while her original field studies could command a substantial fee, there were likely many more people who would pass
through wine country with the desire, but not the means, to
afford the original. So, she created variations of the original
that could be offered in different formats and at different
price points. This variety of levels of offering and a tiered
price structure dramatically expanded the number of people
who not only lusted after, but could afford, her artistry.

Sometimes alternative or submarkets are easy to find, they
literally pop into your head as soon as you plant the seed
and start looking. Other times, it takes a bit more work
and a healthy dose of research and brainstorming. Here are

three online tools I've found immensely useful when brainstorming and researching hotter markets and submarkets.

Bubbl.us

Brainstorming is an essential tool for the career renegade. It allows you to discover solutions and markets that most others miss. One of my favorite approaches to brainstorming is something called "mind-mapping." Mind-mapping allows you to start with a single word, idea, or concept, then visually map out everything that pops into your mind. It's like a flowchart for your brain's creative process and, for someone who is visual, the ability to see what's going on in your mind serves as a great source of new ideas and reveals connections and opportunities.

Bubbl.us is a great free online mind-mapping tool. Try it out, you can teach yourself to use it in less than five minutes and it will very likely become a tool you'll find yourself using to create new ideas on a regular basis. For those of you who'd like to explore mind-mapping software for your computer that is more robust and allows you to create and keep your mind-maps on your own computer, check out Free Mind. It's a free mind-mapping program that works on nearly any computer. You can learn more and download it at www.freemind.sourceforge.net.

Popurls.com

Popurls.com is a website that aggregates what's hot on all the major social media and content-sharing hubs (more detail on these in chapter 15) at any given moment. It's like a snapshot in time of the content that people can't stop talking or e-mailing about and promoting online. Popurls.com also has a search function that allows you to search for a word or keyword phrase contained in the moment's popular content.

While you can certainly add this to your market research arsenal described in chapter 11, I've included it here because I find it equally valuable for the process of brainstorming alternative or submarkets for a passion. You can scan the hundreds of headlines, images, and videos and get a feel for what type of content and issues people are most jazzed about seeing and sharing. This often allows you to integrate a sense of a "pulse of the people" into the very process of brainstorming ways to link your passion to what's hot and turn it loose in more lucrative markets.

Addictomatic.com

Addictomatic.com is much newer than Popurls.com, having launched in early 2008 and, while it shares some functionality, it has a more robust search feature with a longer time span, it includes content from a broader basket of contributors, including conversational media like Twitter .com (more on this in chapter 14), and it is not limited only to the content that has been promoted to the top of the various social-media hubs.

So, when you search on Addictomatic.com for a keyword or phrase, you'll get a much deeper set of results that reach further back in time and are also broken down and visually displayed by the source of the information. The upside over Popurls.com is that you'll get a broader stroke of the conversation. The downside is that you won't get the same sense for what's white-hot right now.

Still, both are great tools to help get a feel for the pulse of the online world, understand who's talking about what, and plant the seeds for creative, higher-demand ways to bring your passion to life in alternative or submarkets that will place a higher value on what you love to do.

FIVE

Got Information? Sell It!

CHANCES ARE, THE JOY YOU get from participating in passion-driven activities comes not only from the activities themselves, but from the culture, community, information, and stuff that surrounds them.

Think about the services and products built around your passion. What about the people and settings that weave through it? Are there ancillary or supporting activities and business opportunities that would keep you close enough to the action to really enjoy what you do but yield a lot more income?

And, most importantly, are there things that either aren't being done or could be done better?

Asking these questions reveals the gaps, places where a need is either not being filled or is screaming for a better solution. And, these are often the places of greatest opportunity, the openings that are ripe for exploitation and monetization.

So, lets look at the major categories of gaps to explore and potentially turn into sources of income, starting with information gaps.

In order to participate in any activity, you need a certain amount of fundamental information. Maybe it's the rules of the game, knowledge of systems, wisdom, cheats, hacks, secrets, and more. If I want to paint, I need to know something about the different types of paints, brushes, canvases, and styles. If I want to build websites, I need to know how to use website-building software, I need to know what the latest trends in design are and understand the critical elements. If I want to be the best hedge-fund lawyer, I need to know not only the law, but the gossip, trends, deal terms, and background as well as the key players.

Oftentimes, the more deeply you get into the activity, the more information you desire. In fact, lack of adequate information often becomes a limiting factor in many activities.

It's not unusual for a secondary market for information to evolve around passion-driven activities that grows into a bigger business than the activity itself. For example, I love to mountain bike, but I also love to know what's going on in the world of mountain biking. And, for this, I read mountain biking magazines.

So, take a look at the activity that makes you come alive and ask the following questions:

- Where do I get my information?
- Is there some information I'd love to have that is hard to find?
- Do enough other people want this information to turn satisfying that demand into a source of income?
- Would there be value in funneling and filtering information?
- Would there be value in compiling or aggregating information?
- Do you have unique insights into the activity or the surrounding culture that would be highly valuable to those looking to excel?
- Do you have information that would solve a problem or facilitate participation?
- Do you have the passion, the depth of knowledge, and the resources to provide that information on a continuing basis?

If you are genuinely passionate about something, chances are pretty good, you already know a lot about it. If you already possess knowledge that others would deeply desire, great. If not, the later chapters on renegade knowledge acquisition and authority building will show you how to build your knowledge base quickly (and with minimal investment), then position yourself as the go-to expert.

Let's look at a number of different ways to exploit and profit from gaps in information.

Research and Reveal Hard-to-Find Information

In nearly every field, there is a class of participants known loosely as mavens. These are generally people who are so passionate about a pursuit, they spend hours immersed in it every day, they talk about it nonstop and devour every bit of knowledge that relates to it. Through a combination of participation, conversation, and study, they often discover bits of information that others in the community would find extremely valuable, especially those who are newer to the activity.

Because people will often pay for information that serves to accelerate their achievement in a passion-driven activity, that information can become a source of substantial revenue when properly revealed and distributed. Bert Ingley's story is the perfect example.

Bert's Story
Revealing Hard-Won Secrets

Anyone who says grown-ups shouldn't be playing video games needs to talk to Bert Ingley. Bert had a serious passion for sports-oriented video games, especially John Madden Football. Supporting a family as a pro-gamer wasn't exactly in the cards, though.

In 2003, Bert discovered a voracious information need and gaping void in the culture surrounding gaming.

It turns out, gamers often play the same game for months, moving on to more challenging levels, and they work tirelessly to find solutions, answers, shortcuts or "hacks" to be able to get to the next level faster. Many were willing to pay to accelerate that process.

Tired of having little control over his career, Bert decided to launch an initiative to teach gamers all the secrets he'd discovered. Rather than teaching online, at seminars, or conferences, though, Bert figured out a way to sell his knowledge to a mass market. He created short insider guides for his favorite sports video games and released them online as e-books.

He started slowly, but within a few years, Bert had not only developed a thriving online community at MaddenTips.com, he was making so much money through his website, he left his full-time job.

By tapping the knowledge that fueled his passion, turning it into publicly available, high-demand information, commoditizing it in the form of booklets, and leveraging the Web as a vehicle for promotion *and distribution (more on this in chapter 9), Bert now earns six-figures online working less than twenty hours a week and spends a ton of time with his wife and kids.*

It all happened because he looked past the specific activity he had a passion for, tapped his unique knowledge of highly desirable information, and discovered an information gap ripe for economic exploitation.

"Now, I'm able to work at home and spend quality time with my wife, two boys, and baby girl," he revealed. "I'm doing something that I love to do and helping other people at the same time. Plus, thanks to automation, I can go on vacation without the whole business grinding to a halt. It's much less stressful than working for someone else."

The more unique, high-demand the information you have to offer the better. If large numbers of people are madly passionate about an activity and you have worked hard to obtain information that will make their pursuit faster, easier, or more enjoyable, you've likely found a viable information gap to exploit.

But, even if you aren't the source of information, there are still alternative ways to exploit gaps in the information that serves your passion.

Funnel, Filter, and Report

We are all stretched for time. Anyone who can deliver the information we hold most dear in the fastest, most efficient format provides value. And, as the pace of life and the volume of information grows, really good funneling, filtering, and reporting becomes increasingly valuable. So valuable, people just might be willing to pay for this service.

Magazine and newspaper editors and radio and television producers have been funneling, filtering, and reporting information and profiting from it for decades. Big deal, no big news there.

What *is* new, however, is the opportunity for Joe and Josephina Citizen to now not only play a similar role, but to turn the need for fast and efficient information into a source of revenue. Gina Trapani is a great example.

Gina's Story •
Code Monkey Turns Tech Editor Extraordinaire

In the early 2000s, Gina Trapani was a code monkey in New York City. Developing the back ends of a host of high-level websites, she would get handed new designs with the instruction, "Build this." While Gina loved the problem-solving aspect of the job, her lack of involvement in the creative process fueled increasing levels of boredom. Until, finally, she couldn't take it anymore. So, heading into the world of freelancing, she turned in her resignation.

"I still remember walking out the door that day," Gina shared, "and thinking, 'I'm free! This is great! . . . Oh, crap!'"

The next few years were filled with a lot of exploring, while Gina sustained herself through a variety of freelance technology jobs. The perceived security of a nine-to-five coding job kept tempting her to go back to her production-driven past. It wasn't easy to resist the siren call of a lucrative fallback, but she remained committed to figuring out the bigger picture.

Then, in late 2005, Gina stumbled into an opportunity that brought everything together. She married her love of coding and maven's quest for knowledge about everything tech with her less public, though lifelong, love of writing. The opportunity just clicked.

She joined Gawker Media to launch Lifehacker.com, an online community revolving around the intersection between technology, productivity, and lifestyles. Gina and the Lifehacker.com gang spend massive amounts of time digesting information from thousands of sources, filtering out the 95 percent of the information that isn't relevant, then reporting the information that is most useful in a single place.

Now a little more than three years old Lifehacker.com is read by millions of people every month and Gina's role as the founding editor, tech-maven, and chief filter, funnel, and aggregator has led to two subsequent books, Lifehacker: 88 Tech Tips to Turbocharge Your Day and Upgrade Your Life.

Gina's living as a technology-writer, editor, and purveyor of information has equaled, if not significantly outstripped, her living as a code monkey.

"Here's the thing," Gina revealed, "you do the thing you can't not do." Read that sentence again. It took me a couple of passes before the power of it sank in. Gina loved to code, but she was able to satisfy her tech jones, serve her love of the surrounding community and passion for writing, and earn a great living not by coding, but by funneling, filtering, and reporting information for that very community.

Aggregate and Disseminate

Effectively funneling and filtering massive amounts of information and reporting the gems provides huge value, but there's another information-management service that also makes peoples' lives easier and often provides fertile ground for exploitation—aggregation and compiling.

David's Story
Sales Exec Turned Personal Growth Aggregator

Rolling into the 1990s, David Riklan was cruising along his high-level career in enterprise technology sales. He was bright, respected, made a nice living, and was building a family. And, every day he went to work was a day he wanted desperately to be doing something else. His day-to-day activities and the company's bigger mission did little to inspire him and the culture and setting he'd landed in were slowly wearing him down. Around that same time, the Internet was beginning to gather steam. David was fascinated by what was happening online. He was sure it was going to be huge.

So, in 1996, he launched a side business, SelfGrowth.com. Within a few years, the website generated enough additional income to bolster David's full-time sales salary nicely. And, with his family growing, every dollar was needed.

But after about four and a half years, David's dual life was beginning to bump up against the limitations of his waking energy.

He reached a point where he felt like something had to give. He fantasized about making SelfGrowth.com his sole source of income, but also knew it would require a far greater investment of time to take it to that next level. Then fate stepped in when his employer hit a rough patch and David was presented with a one-time buy-out offer: Take the money and run or stay and change positions. It was a moment of reckoning.

He wanted desperately to take the package and use the money to buy himself the chance to work on SelfGrowth.com full time. He knew, though, that he'd need to grow it big enough to cover both the income lost from his full-time job and the revenue currently generated by the site. The family needed all of it to live. And, he'd need to do it before the cushion from his buy-out package was depleted. That was a massive challenge. And it set the tone for a series of heartfelt, emotional discussions between David and his wife.

The site was still growing nicely, but at nowhere near the rate it would need to grow for it to be able to support the family in a matter of months. David needed a big idea, something that could vault his new venture to the next level. He wracked his brain. But nothing was coming. So he committed to learning more about the top people in the field of self-help and personal development. He began looking for a book that catalogued each person and provided an overview of their philosophies, history, and publications. He looked everywhere, but couldn't find it. The lightbulb went on.

He'd found the giant gap in an industry flooded with players and information.

Over the next few months, David compiled a comprehensive directory and gave it a name, Self-Improvement: The Top 101 Experts That Help Us Improve Our Lives.

David then ran an e-mail campaign that a number of authors had begun to use to make their books instant Amazon bestsellers to promote the launch of his e-book.

David's fantasy was to sell ten thousand e-books in the first year. What unfolded, though, blew his mind and launched his business, for real.

Within minutes of going live with his e-book promotional campaign, sales exploded. Twenty-four hours later, four thousand books were sold, generating over $100,000 in revenue, almost all of it profit. Building on this success, he repeated the campaign every month over a number of months and sold thousands more e-books, to the tune of hundreds of thousands of dollars.

SelfGrowth.com was now a reality, a business driven by passion that was capable of comfortably supporting David's family. In the years since releasing that first book, the website has spawned more Web portals, a series of newsletters that go out to more than nine hundred thousand subscribers, and David has written and published a number of other books, all available for both download and in printed form.

David wanted information desperately, but couldn't find it anywhere; he did find an information gap. There was no single resource that compiled information about the leading figures in personal growth. He figured that if he wanted this resource, others with an interest in personal development would want it too. Once assembled, he then leveraged technology to produce, market, and distribute it for little money. David's story is a great example of the power of aggregating, compiling, and distributing information in a discrete, easy-to-digest format.

Leveraging Technology Turns Information into Income

As we saw in chapter 3, there are many ways to turn information into income. Once you've uncovered an information gap, the question becomes how best to test and then exploit that gap. There are thousands of pages in books, blogs, and beyond on this very topic, so here is a brief introduction to the top four vehicles, along with resources to learn more about each:

Create Books, e-Books, and Other Downloadable Info Products

E-books can range in size from about twenty-five pages (anything smaller is more likely a newsletter or booklet) to hundreds of pages. You can write an e-book in MS

Word or your preferred word-processing program, then save it in PDF format, which is a document format that reproduces well across all types of computer-operating systems and platforms. Publishers have attached various encryption schemes over the years in an attempt to stop people from sharing their content without payment or permission, with varying degrees of success.

If you are a writer, write the content yourself. If not, you can find people to write it for you relatively inexpensively, using the resources that follow. Once you have your e-book written, give it to a few friends whom you trust to edit it, and spend the time to craft it into something that (a) delivers high-value content, and (b) is easy to read. When the content is ready for primetime, here are three common ways to automate the process of making it available for sale:

Post it on your website: If you already have a website or blog, you can post your e-book for download there. Generally, you would add a page with the cover image, table of contents, possibly a free sample chapter, and a buy-now button that links to PayPal or another payment service. Once you confirm payment, you can then e-mail a link to a second page that allows the buyer to download their copy (or set the system up to do this automatically). The benefit of this approach is tight control over your content and the ability to keep all the revenue over and above PayPal's fees.

The downside is the marketing burden. It is completely up to you to drive people to your webpage to buy the e-book.

Post it on ClickBank.com: Sign up as a merchant at ClickBank.com, upload your e-book file, take a look at similar offerings, and price it competitively. The benefit of making your product available at ClickBank is that thousands of ClickBank affiliates (websites that look for other products to advertise and sell in exchange for a commission) can then find your e-book and post advertisements and links to it on their websites and e-newsletters. This can dramatically expand your marketing reach. The downside is that these affiliates often expect a sizable commission, in the neighborhood of 50 percent of the sale price. But, remember, with an e-book, once it's written, there are essentially no production or delivery costs, leaving the remaining 50 percent almost entirely as profit.

Post it and make it available as a print book at Lulu.com: I've seen more and more people turning to Lulu.com to handle their book and e-book publishing needs lately. Lulu, which is very well trafficked these days, allows you to upload and design a beautiful book and list it for sale online either as a printed book or e-book. There is no setup fee, they host your book's content and handle the sales transactions, and you collect a substantial percentage of the revenue (80 percent as of this writing). You can also have your e-book formatted for the iPhone or Sony e-book reader. And, because it's featured in the Lulu.com catalogue, there is an added marketing benefit to using Lulu.com to create, test, and then sell your information product.

Audio/Video Format

Information is increasingly being conveyed in audio and video format. Anyone can upload video to one of the online video-publishing websites like YouTube.com, Google .com, Revver.com, and others. And, audio content can be recorded and uploaded to websites like Audible or made available as podcasts through Apple's iTunes platform. This content, though is generally free content. So, it is great to use as *teaser* for paid content, but you'll need a different way to handle paid audio and video content delivery. Lulu.com, again, offers a nice suite of services and we'll go into more detail in the next section on exploiting education gaps.

Monetize Online or Digital Content

Hands down, the fastest, easiest way to get your content in front of a lot of people is through a blog. A blog is simply a website that is structured as a series of regularly updated articles or posts, though blogging platforms are now so robust, they permit far more than this. I will discuss the process of setting up a blog and leveraging it for marketing and buzz in detail in chapter 14.

The question always arises: How do blogs make money? The cold hard fact is, most don't. But that is more about a lack of understanding about how to launch and grow a blog capable of generating revenue than a true inability to make it happen.

Blogs make money in one of two ways (or sometimes, both).

Direct Monetization: If you build your blog around the desire to offer the type of high-value information we've been discussing, you will begin to draw attention and traffic to your blog. Once you have enough traffic (generally a minimum of five hundred visits a day), you can:

- Place advertisements on your blog, by negotiating rates directly with companies who want exposure to your readers.
- Accept sponsors for certain content.
- Sign up as a publisher with Google Adsense and allow Google to serve their ads on your blog and collect a percentage of the revenue every time someone clicks on an ad.
- Contact one of the growing number of blog advertis-

ing companies (FederatedMedia.net, TTZMedia .com, BlogAds.com, and Izea.com are the big ones) and get paid to serve ads or write reviews for the advertisers they represent.

How much you can earn with each of these is a factor of how well you choose your niche, how valuable the information you provide is, how much traffic you have, and how willing you are to treat the entire adventure as a business. While many bloggers don't make much money through blogging, that is not so much a function of lack of opportunity as it is a lack of knowledge or willingness to invest a concerted effort into launching and building a blog with the intent to generate a substantial living. Indeed, a number of bloggers mentioned in this book earn a solid living from on-blog advertising and sponsorship.

The websites and books listed in chapter 14 will help you dramatically accelerate this process with a wealth of tools, tips, and techniques, but the go-to resources are Darren Rowse's ProBlogger.net and his book *ProBlogger: Secrets for Blogging Your Way to a Six-Figure Income,* written along with fellow pro-blogger and new media consultant, Chris Garret (www.Chrisg.com).

Indirect monetization: In addition to income generated directly from your blog's content, you can leverage the authority created by your blog to generate income in a myriad of different ways:

- Create a premium content area, charge a subscription, and offer a higher level of content, interaction, and direct access to your expertise through e-mail, teleseminars, or webinars.

- Place a *Hire Me* page on your blog and offer services related to the information you share on the blog. At Chrisg.com and Remarkablogger.com you'll find links for consulting services. ChrisBrogan.com and StevePavlina.com have pages dedicated to speaking, and IttyBiz.com has a "Hire IttyBiz" link that takes the reader to a page about small business marketing services. Explore all these blogs, they are great examples of how to leverage online expertise into off-blog income.

- Partner with other bloggers or aggregate other bloggers into a network, serve ads across all blogs in the network, and take a percentage of the revenue. After creating two highly successful, blogs, ProBlogger .net's Rowse did this, creating B5Media, a network of more than three hundred blogs. Similarly, Spark plugging.com CEO Wendy Piersall recently turned her work-at-home blog into a growing network and career-columnist and author Penelope Trunk recently grew her career-blogging brand into a full-on network at BrazenCareerist.com.

- But, the big, *big,* BIG one, the opportunity only a handful of bloggers have tapped, is the ability to market complementary products and services that you genuinely believe are worthy purchases to your list of readers and subscribers.

In direct marketing, the single most important element of any campaign is the list. You can have a great product or service, fabulous marketing and copywriting, but if your list of prospects is poorly qualified or cold, meaning they have not had regular contact with you or received valuable information on an ongoing basis, the likelihood of the campaign succeeding drops dramatically. Knowing this, Internet marketers have taken list building and list "warming" through regular contact to the level of an art form.

When it comes to blogging, your list is comprised of your readers and subscribers. You grow that list by delivering valuable content, and each time you do that it serves a secondary marketing purpose. It warms your list and makes the people on it more receptive to recommendations.

Recently, a small handful of Internet marketers and bloggers have begun to tap the blended power of direct marketing and blogging, launching products by marketing them to their blogging audiences and subscribers. Recent examples include:

- CopyBlogger.com's Brian Clark, who launched his Teaching Sells paid membership site through his blog, enrolling hundreds of members within weeks.
- ProBlogger.net's Darren Rowse and ChrisG.com's Chris Garret announced the publication of their book, *ProBlogger: Secrets for Blogging Your Way to a Six-Figure Income* (Wiley, 2008) on their blogs a month before the publication date and pre-sold a good part of the first printing within twenty-four hours.
- ZenHabits.net's Leo Babauta launched his *Zen to Done* e-book through his blog and thousands of copies were purchased and downloaded in the first month alone.
- DuctTapeMarketing.com's John Jantsch launched a series of marketing mixed-media kits and published a book.

   You'll learn more about Brian and John in the next section on tapping educational gaps.

A word of warning before you wade into these waters, though. The blogosphere runs on a lot of unwritten rules and there is a longstanding ethic based on respecting your readers and giving more than you get. So, before you begin blogging for bucks, recommending products or leveraging your list, spend some time blogging, learn the rules of the game, and give away a ton of valuable content. Never directly promote anything, unless you believe it is worth the investment and, if you have a financial interest in something you're promoting, disclose it. Be transparent. Even then, there will be a segment of bloggers who will strongly reject any attempt to commercialize or monetize your blog. Consider yourself warned.

E-newsletters: Rather than releasing your information on an ongoing basis on a blog or website, certain less time-sensitive content can work well in a downloadable or e-mailed newsletter format. David Riklan from SelfGrowth .com offers a lot of great content on his main website, but also boasts more than nine hundred thousand subscribers to a variety of e-newsletters. Each of these newsletters features advertisements, which, in addition to his books and e-books, generate a significant source of ongoing revenue. Resources to learn how to create and manage e-newsletters include AWeber.com, ConstantContact.com, and Topica .com.

SIX

Want to Teach?
Expand Your Reach

COULD YOU TAKE AN ACTIVITY you are madly passionate about and teach it? Could you partner with others to make it happen? And, most importantly: *Is there an educational gap you can exploit to bring your passion to life in the form of teaching?*

Before you respond, "Yes, but I wouldn't make enough money doing it," let's take a look at Bette's story.

Bette's Story
Artist Mom Clones Herself to Teach 30,000

Graduating with a BFA in fine arts and a passion for drawing, Bette Fetter quickly discovered the challenge of earning a living as an artist.

Without mega-connections or a giant name, just paying her rent, let alone making a real living, seemed near impossible.

A few years later, married with kids, Bette turned her energy to being a mom and wife full time. But, her artistic side never left her. Indeed, she had a strong desire to share her passion for art with her kids. So, she began to teach them. But what began as a simple desire to share her love of art turned into something she never imagined.

Every week, Bette's kids would circle around her kitchen table to do art. Over time, her kids were joined by a growing pack of friends for their weekly classes. Before long, there was no room left at the table. So Bette created a more organized weekly art program for kids and began to charge for it. With schools cutting back on their arts programs, word quickly spread and demand for Bette's classes quickly grew beyond what she could handle.

She realized if she wanted to keep the program going, she'd have to multiply herself. So, she began to teach people how to teach art in her very special way and formed a company, Young Rembrandts. Still, demand for her programming kept outstripping what her team could provide, so she eventually decided to take her teaching jones to a whole new level, turning Young Rembrandts into a full-blown franchise.

From humble beginnings, teaching neighborhood kids around her kitchen table, she's now grown a virtual children's art empire, with more than sixty franchises that teach art to some thirty thousand kids a week. In fact, Young Rembrandts grew so quickly, it wasn't long before Bette's husband quit his full-time sales job to go work for his wife.

What started as a lifelong passion for something that could never pay the bills turned into a profitable business teaching art to kids.

And, along the way, Bette discovered a second passion for the business of teaching artists how to earn a living by teaching art to kids. It turns out this seemingly left-brain, ultra-creative artist has not only an aptitude for but a love of business too.

We'll explore more on franchising versus licensing later in this chapter. Training others to do what you do, though, isn't the only way to turn your teaching jones into way more money than the average teacher makes.

Tap Media and Technology to Teach Thousands While You Sleep

What if you could teach something once, then have thousands of students around the world enjoy your instruction twenty-four hours a day, seven days a week? And pay for it! With advances in home-media software, cameras, technology, and the rapid expansion of high-speed Internet access, you can now make money teaching in your pajamas more easily than ever before.

John's Story
Marketing Guru Turns to Virtual Teaching

Small-business marketing guru, blogger, and author John Jantsch spent his days immersed in the marketing needs of his clients. He knew their struggles, their desires, their challenges and successes. And, over time, this experience began to reveal a wide-scale educational gap that was ripe for the tapping.

Small businesses were caught in a squeeze. They were desperate for sensible, cost-effective, proven ways to market their businesses and for people to help them implement effective solutions and campaigns. But most did not have the funds to go to a larger marketing or advertising firm for help, so they did what they could in-house and used the local copy or print shop to create the final product.

John saw an opportunity to create an affordable course on small-business marketing, delivered as a series of lessons, in the form of printed materials, audio CDs, and DVDs. Leveraging his growing reputation as a small-business expert and the founder of the Duct TapeMarketing.com blog, he launched his Ultimate Marketing System, a mixed-media marketing education and implementation system with more than four hundred pages of printed material and a dozen audio CDs.

Knowing that many people would want help putting the information into action, he also created an affordable distance telephone coaching program. And, true to his strong emphasis on getting small businesses to tap the marketing potential of the Web, he used his blog, along with a variety of Internet marketing tools and techniques to bring his products and services to a mass small-business market. This led to the publication of Duct Tape Marketing, *the book, in 2006 and an ever-expanding line of products and services.*

Brian's Story
Marketer Creates Interactive Learning Environments

Seeing the convergence of online education and blogging coming a few years back, lawyer turned Internet marketer and copywriter Brian Clark took action. In early 2006, he launched CopyBlogger.com, a blog dedicated to teaching bloggers how to write compelling online copy. He then leveraged social media to help grow his audience rapidly, generating a huge following and a nice secondary income from the blog.

But, that was just the beginning for Brian. The longstanding ethic of the blogosphere is to give away your knowledge and make money either through advertising, sponsorship, affiliate programs, or by leveraging your authority off-blog. But, with his background in Internet market-ing, Brian was well versed in another option, packaging high-value "premium" content into paid online membership sites called interactive learning environments.

He'd done this himself many times in the past and he developed a strong desire to share what he had learned. So, in 2007, he created Teaching Sells, a paid membership program that teaches people how to leverage a deep passion for expertise or even interest in a subject into a paid online learning system that generates revenue twenty-four hours a day, seven days a week.

Brian then tapped his giant blog audience to launch Teaching Sells and, since then, has had the benefit of teaching his approach to more *than one thousand people (at up to $97 per month), getting their feed-back and constantly refining and optimizing the system.*

Brian shared some critical insights into the process:

- You do *not* need to be a known expert to make this work. In fact, very often the most accomplished "practitioners" make the worst teachers. It's enough to have a strong interest in or passion for a particular activity or the culture that supports that community. If you're not the expert, your job essentially becomes that of a director, facilitator, and promoter. You source the experts, work with them to develop a curriculum or product, shape and produce the educational content, create an online presence to host the content and manage students, and then promote the program. You do all this in exchange for a percentage.

- You do not need a following to make it work. While Brian launched Teaching Sells largely through his substantial blogging audience, you do *not* need a massive group of followers to succeed. Indeed, if you create a service that has enough value and you can demonstrate a strong demand for the knowledge you'll be sharing, you'll very likely be able to partner with people who already have giant lists in exchange for a percentage of the revenue (often 50 percent) generated by subscribers from their lists. This is how nearly every large Internet marketing product is launched.

- You can do it in your spare time. Building, launching, and growing an online teaching system can be done on a part-time basis with very little investment. So you can keep your day job and grow your educational-subscription business on the side until it has enough legs for you to make the bigger jump.

Test Before You Invest

As we saw with Bette Fetter and her Young Rembrandts franchise journey, it is possible to multiply yourself and earn a sizable income, too. Instruction that requires a lot of hands-on attention and direct interaction or programs tailored toward kids are often best expanded through more traditional offline means, like franchising or licensing, but the long arm of technology is making it possible to teach more and more complex hands-on content online.

Before you go down the teach and multiply path though, it's important to:

- Start with a content area to teach that is a manifestation of your passion, then, if possible, create a simple lesson plan or course structure, bring it to life locally, get feedback, and refine and test the interest in your own community. Make sure your product, service, or concept has all the kinks worked out *before* you look to expand it. Growing too early can be as deadly as not growing at all.

- Do it long enough to make sure there is strong, enduring local interest. You don't want to multiply a business that has not yet proven successful and shown strong, lasting demand. It might take anywhere from six months to a few years to prove the enduring nature of your concept.

- Consider whether what people are responding to will have a broader market interest. What works in a small town in Texas might not fly in New England, for example. Use your own experience, resources, and contacts as well as some of the tools and techniques in chapter 11 to test this.

Then, if all the above factors point to a strong desire for what you'd like to teach, it's time to explore leveraging business expansion, franchising, licensing, or technology to effectively clone yourself and earn a lot more money than your average solo teacher.

Producing Educational Content that Makes People Happy They Paid for It

Regardless of the vehicle you choose to package, manufacture, distribute, and charge for your course materials, you need to create an intelligent lesson and you need to write, record, and produce high-value, professional-looking materials.

Once you believe you have discovered an education gap that jibes with your passion and will translate well to some combination of video, audio, and print, the next step is to create your course materials. This is generally a three-step process.

The Three-Step Process to Creating Your Course Material

1. *Create a course objective, outline, and individual lesson plans.* Write out the big-picture educational objective. Then break it into short, easy-to-digest bits of knowledge. Try to estimate what can be taught in fifteen- to thirty-minute bites, then turn those bites into individual lesson plans.
2. *Decide which content is best delivered in which format.* Some content will work well in print, and other content might work better as audio, but more visually oriented or complex content might be best

presented in video format. If what you are teaching revolves around using a computer, you may also want to include something called screen-capture audio/video, which allows you to record what is happening on your computer screen and add an audio track to talk people through it.

3. *Produce the content.* Written content is the easiest to produce, using a basic word processing program. If you don't have Microsoft Word, try Google's free online word-processor, Google Documents at www .docs.Google.com. Then, create a basic script from your lesson plan and use a digital video camera to record the classes. You can even do most or all of the editing and production on your home computer (see the resources below).

Below, you'll find a bunch of resources for everything from helping to write written content and lesson plans to creating compelling video, setting up paid membership sites, manufacturing, packaging, and distributing mixed-media versions of your educational content. So, take some time to explore these resources, feel out which approach seems best, and then start teaching.

Here are some specialized resources for course creation, lesson planning, media product creation, production, and marketing:

Course/Lesson Planning

Teach-nology.com/tutorials/teaching/lesson_plan/: Walks you through the steps and critical considerations in creating your lesson plans.

Teach-nology.com/web_tools/lesson_plan/: Online form allows you to create your own lesson plan, then generate a printable version.

www.TeachingSells.com: Comprehensive program that teaches all aspects of online course creation and delivery.

Writing

If you'd rather not do the writing, you should be able to find someone else to do it for you by posting a description of your needs on any number of freelance writing websites, including:

- elance.com
- freelanceswitch.com
- guru.com
- scriptlance.com
- ifreelance.com, or even
- Craigslist.com

Printed Material Production

Staples or FedEx/Kinkos: You can do the printing at home for the first go-around or bring your files to Staples or FedEx/Kinkos to copy and bind into nicer looking finished products. Even though I have a pretty high-end setup at home, I generally go the extra mile to have my materials finished outside, because people subconsciously assign value based not only on the content of the educational materials, but on their appearance.

Lulu.com: Depending on the nature of your printed materials, Lulu.com may be a good resource to turn your content into a book, manual e-book, or PDF. In fact, their ability to make your content available in multiple formats and handle the hosting and sales transactions makes Lulu.com an appealing option.

48HourPrint.com: This is a resource I've used many times for smaller promotional jobs, but they are also capable of printing more substantial materials, including booklets up to forty-eight pages.

Duplication, Packaging, Warehousing, Order Taking, and Distribution/Shipping for Audio CDs, DVDs, and Mixed-Media Products

DVDBaby.com: This is a full-service company that offers DVD and CD duplication (higher per item cost, but no minimum), replication (less per unit cost/minimum required), and packaging.

Disk.com: This company offers reasonably priced and reliable production, duplication (fewer than 250 DVDs/higher price per DVD), replication (250 or more/less expensive), packaging, warehousing, order fulfillment, and shipping. A wide range of options and levels of website order integration.

Video Editing and Production

Camtasia (www.Camtasia.com): Camtasia is screen-capture software that allows you to record what you are doing on your computer screen and add audio for Windows-based computers.

ScreenFlow (www.varasoftware.com/products/screenflow/): ScreenFlow is similar to Camtasia, but it's available for Apple OS computers.

StomperVision (www.stompernet.net/stompervision): On-line video course details everything from basic equipment to scripting, using screen-capture software, creating video that is both educational and promotional and getting it ready for online use or distribution as DVDs.

OnlineVideoToolkit.com: Great collection of free online videos on everything from equipment to editing, lighting, and publishing.

Video editing and production for Apple users: iMovie and iDVD are great programs to edit, master, and produce small quantities on your own home computer. Final Cut and Final Cut Pro are the step-up semi-pro and pro-level programs. These are great, especially to test market and get viewer feedback. The former two programs are fairly easy to learn how to use, but the learning curve grows once you move to the latter two, more robust programs.

Video editing and production for PC users: Adobe Premiere Elements seems to be taking a leading role in consumer-level PC video editing software. You might also consider Pinnacle Studio or Avid (www.pinnaclysys.com). Pinnacle is the consumer-level product, while Avid is the pro-level.

Resources to Clone Your Inner Teacher

Business Expansion, Franchising, and Licensing

When demand for Bette Fetter's art classes began to outstrip the number of classes she could teach, her first step was to start training others to teach her content and format, then send them out into the world as her representatives. She could have kept growing the organization that way. The benefit would be her ability to control all aspects of the business as it grew, but that benefit is also a burden. It would mean heading up an increasingly larger organization with a lot of time spent on administration and management. Plus, Bette believed it was important to empower each person with the opportunity to own their own businesses, while benefiting from her systems, brand, and support.

This led her to explore franchising and licensing, both of which are vehicles to accomplish a similar task. With franchising, you give someone else permission to use your business systems, products, services, training, brand/trademark, and marketing in exchange for a fee. You may also grant them an exclusive territory. Usually, there is an upfront fee that covers a certain amount of initial training and a number of monthly fees that often include a share of each franchisee's monthly revenue.

For example, someone interested in becoming a Young

Rembrandts franchisee would pay an initial fee of $31,500, a royalty of 8 to 10 percent of revenue, and expect to invest between $39,500 and $48,800 to get the business going (check the website for recent information).

To become a franchisor or seller of franchises, in most states, you must prepare and, depending on the state, file a document called a Uniform Franchise Offering Circular, or UFOC. This is a big document that takes a lot of work and, often, substantial legal fees to complete and file with the appropriate agencies. You'll also need to create an operating manual that details every aspect of the way you run your business.

Licensing is generally more limited and much less burdensome to implement. With licensing, you give someone else the right to offer certain of your branded products or services. Sometimes that includes the use of your brand. Other times it may even include the right to manufacture and sell your products or services in exchange for a fee. This is where the line between franchising and licensing can get pretty blurry. In fact, in many states, they are so closely defined, it is difficult to know exactly which structure you are exploring.

What is clear, though, is that the initial registration and annual filing requirements tend to be substantially more involved and costly for franchisors than for licensors. This very fact leads many businesses to try to structure their growth to avoid being deemed a franchise.

I've actually gone through the entire franchising process myself and, even as a former securities lawyer, I have to admit to finding it a bit daunting.

Here are some resources that will go a long way toward explaining the basics of franchising and licensing. Before you begin to travel too far down cither road, though, I'd strongly encourage you to speak with an attorney and/or consultant who specializes in franchising and licensing. Done right, both paths can be immensely profitable; done wrong, they can result in a lot of distress and a big, fat mess.

Franchising and Licensing Resources

Franchise.com

FranchiseTimes.com and *Franchise Times* magazine

Franchise.org

FranchisePundit.com

FranchiseLawBlog.com

FranchisePerfection.com/blog

TheFranchiseKing.typepad.com

FranchiseGator.com

FranchiseDirect.com/blog

Wipo.int/sme/en/documents/franchising.htm

http://www.huizenga.nova.edu/ExecEd/IIFE/
default.cfm

Franchise-chat.com

Ftc.gov/bcp/franchise/netfran.shtm

Entrepreneur.com

*Franchising and Licensing: Two Powerful Ways to
Grow Your Business in Any Economy* by Andrew J.
Sherman (Amacon, 2004)

*Franchise Bible: How to Buy a Franchise or Franchise
Your Own Business,* 6th ed., by Erwin J. Keup
(Entreprenuer Press, 2007)

Tap Technology to Grow Your Teaching Empire

Traditional business structures are one way to turn
your desire to teach your passion into a far greater income
than normal. But, over the last five years, technology has
opened doors that were never open to the average individual
in this area.

We can now produce an entire educational program with
a home computer and, if needed, a video camera, then have
it reproduced, packaged, sold, and delivered online for a
relatively modest fee. We can turn it into real hard products
or keep it entirely virtual. And, we can sell our educational

solutions not only in our local communities, but all over the world, every hour of every day. The Internet has become our grand production, marketing, sales, and delivery partner and, here's the really cool thing—it never sleeps.

Educational Mixed-Media Products and Services

As we saw with Duct Tape Marketing's John Jantsch, a great way to satisfy your passion for a particular niche is to fill an educational gap with a mixed-media product (MMP). An MMP is simply a course or collection of lessons that has been packaged into a mixed-media format. It often includes audio CDs, a printed manual, video DVDs, and other relevant specialized materials.

Teach and Make Money Online

Creating MMPs isn't the only way to leverage technology and media formats to cash in on your teaching passion. Once recorded, edited, and produced, you can also place the very same material online, either on a blog or traditional website, for public viewing for free, and then profit from it by serving relevant ads alongside the educational content.

A second, similar option is the growing opportunity to post your high-value educational content on how-to/entertainment video-hosting websites that allow you to share in the revenues generated by content that is viewed often. A great example of this is Metacafe.com's Producer Rewards program (www.metacafe.com/producer_rewards).

Metacafe.com is a video-sharing website that features very short videos. Through its Producer Rewards program, video producers can submit video and, if chosen, earn $5 per one thousand views. That might not sound like much, but, for those who put a serious effort into creating content that is professionally produced, entertaining, valuable, and speaks to a large number of people, the returns can really add up.

In fact, producing a series of ninety-four brief "edutainment" videos (videos that entertain, while educating), Florida-based Kip Kedersha pulled in more than $100,000 from Metacafe.com in the past year alone. Maintaining rights to his content, he can still use it to generate revenue anywhere else he likes. Granted, Kedersha's earning led the pack by a wide margin, but, as I always say, I believe that's more about knowledge and drive than ability.

Take a look at Kedersha's "KipKay" channel over at Metacafe.com to view his videos. Look at what he's doing, note how he films, scripts, chooses his subjects, and produces his videos. Now I wonder what might happen if you used your market research tools to find out what subject areas were getting massive traffic and buzz on a given day, matched it up with something you were passionate about, cranked out a two-minute edutainment video, and posted it on Metacafe.com.

Are the wheels spinning yet?!

Subscription-Based Online Learning Portals

Folks, we're still not done with ways to take those educational audio and video files, PDFs, and manuals and turn them into money online. Remember Brian Clark? The lawyer turned Internet marketer turned Copyblogger.com blogger and Teaching Sells paid membership site guy? You know, the one with one thousand people paying him between $30 and $97 a month to read lessons and watch videos and interact with each other in an effort to essentially learn how to be him?

While Brian Clark didn't invent the concept of subscription-based interactive learning environments (ILEs), he has been highly successful at both creating them and developing a comprehensive program that teaches others how to create them around educational content they are passionate about. ILEs offer another great way to distribute your educational content online.

While it takes more effort up front to set up a private website that hosts your educational content, the fact that you never have to pay to manufacture, package, or ship an actual product more than makes up for this very quickly.

Leveraging technology allows anyone with a high-speed Internet connection and a basic computer to participate in the learning experience, regardless of location.

And it moves people into an automated payment system that bills their credit cards every month. Psychologically, this is a huge change. It shifts the burden away from you having to resell to students every time you come out with new content. Instead, your students have to opt out to avoid paying for new content.

This approach is not without challenges for you, however. In order to inspire students to stay subscribed, you have the burden of producing a continuing stream of high-value, fresh, entertaining, and educational content every single month for the life of the program. Or, you can just make the entire program a fixed length, like six months and recommend that people view certain lessons on a weekly basis and complete exercises and homework to prepare for the following week's lesson.

You also have the option of mixing in live video or tele-seminars on a regular basis that allows for regular question and answer sessions. The rule of thumb is, the more live interaction they get with you, the higher the monthly fee.

Here is a short list of specialized resources to explore getting started with subscription-based interactive learning environments:

TeachingSells.com: Brian Clark's membership site that teaches people how to create paid membership sites.

CNX.org: Hub for people looking to collaborate in creating educational materials.

Entrepreneurs-Journey.com: Blog run by blogger and Internet marketer Yaro Starak. Similar to Brian, Yaro launched a membership site that teaches people how to make money blogging before moving more heavily into wider-scale Internet marketing. Lots of great info available for free.

MembershipSiteAdvisor.com: Offers extensive information and case studies on membership site creation and marketing, available in the form of a membership site with a free trial.

aMember.com: Membership management system.

CopyBlogger.com: Brian Clark's main blog, where he shares a wealth of copywriting and marketing information.

SEVEN

Exploit the Need for Stuff

VERY OFTEN, THAT THING WE most love to do also requires a certain amount of *stuff*. Beaders need beads, bead boards, thread, crimps, and more. Rock climbers need harnesses, shoes, chocks, nuts, cams, and beyond. It's not unusual for an entire, equally passionate subculture to evolve around that gear. If you look deep enough, you can often find gaps in demand for the gear, stuff, or "schwag" that supports the main activities.

Sometimes those gaps are in the way gear is being provided; other times, they revolve around limitations in selection; and sometimes, you'll even find a gap where either no product yet exists or what does exist can be greatly improved upon. Exploiting these gaps and bundling them with service or community often provides fertile ground for economic opportunity. This was the case with Susan Nichols and her creation of the Skidless yoga mat cover.

Susan's Story
Yogini Finds Opportunity in Slip-Free Yoga Mats

Susan was a longtime student of a very dynamic, physical style of yoga known as Ashtanga. In Ashtanga, you sweat. A lot. That sweat ends up on your mat, which is often a rubbery, not very absorbent surface that becomes very slippery when wet. This is a real challenge in certain poses and leads to frequent slippage on the mat and frustration.

As Ashtanga morphed into other dynamic styles that have become more widely practiced, the problem of mat slippage has affected a bigger and bigger market. Various solutions came to market, but none seemed to work very well. So, passionate about yoga and fueled to find a solution that would make the practice more enjoyable both for herself and for the larger community, Susan began to work on her own answer.

At the time, she worked as an art director at a toy manufacturer, so she was familiar with the creative process, how to design and create prototypes, and how to test a product. She began to brainstorm products that might provide a stable surface, while not interfering with the practice's organic flow.

She'd tried nearly everything, when the answer came to her in the form of a microfiber towel to absorb moisture with small rubbery dimples on the bottom to stop slippage. She got to work creating a proto-type and, eventually, through what she describes as one of many karmic moments, she met someone who owned a factory in Asia and was able to produce exactly what she wanted.

A few weeks later, with her prototype in hand, Susan began to show it around, let her friends practice on it, and get feedback. The response was tremendous. Everyone loved the product. It solved the problem bet-ter than anything else on the market. Plus, with her background in art direction, she'd also created packaging with a lot of retail appeal.

To move forward, Susan would need to have one thousand pieces manufactured. That was the bare minimum. It was time to take a leap of faith. So, she borrowed money from someone she knew to open her new company, Yogitoes, and pay for her first order of Skidless mats.

A few months later, the first shipment arrived and Susan began to take it around to various studios and retail stores to sell. The packag-ing was so attractive and the product was so effective, people couldn't stop talking about it, and that first shipment sold out in the blink of an eye. Within six months her start-up loan was paid back in full, and her company was poised to grow.

Today, Susan oversees a staff of thirteen people, with multiple products and international distribution and sales. Yogitoes is so success-ful, Susan has been approached by venture capital firms and prospective suitors, but she's turned them all down. She makes a great living, but what's more important to her is that she makes that living in service to the community and the practice she adores. She loves yoga, she loves serving the yoga community, and she has even leveraged her company as *a vehicle to serve and donate to a variety of children's causes around the world.*

Susan's ability to mine a gear gap and turn it into a serious source of income started with her identification of a need that wasn't being served in her own experience of the activity that was her consuming passion. She then noticed that same gap in the broader community of people who practice yoga.

The first wave of market research, for her, consisted largely of her own experience, observation, and conversations with those in the local community. This inspired her to put the time in to research ways to create a product that would solve the problem. Once the prototype was in hand, she took the physical product and tested it in a similar manner. The positive response gave her the confidence to invest in the product and bring it to the broader market. The speed at which the first order of one thousand pieces sold out then provided additional confirmation and emboldened her to make bigger investments and grow that initial product into a brand with multiple products, serving similar needs.

Prototype, Manufacture, or License

If the renegade path you are exploring requires you to create a product to fill a perceived gap in a marketplace, how do you actually *make* a product?

As we've already seen, the first step is generally to create a prototype of your product. Start with drawings and descriptions. Do your best to define exactly what your product should look like, how it should work, what it should do, and what it should be made of. If you don't have the drawing or descriptive skills to create a fairly good representation of the product you'd like to create, you may want to explore working with an illustrator, designer, or technical writer. Start with personal referrals and, if you strike out, then try the freelance sites listed in chapter 6.

Once you have this step complete, if you believe your idea has serious financial potential and it would be easy to knock off once public, you may want to bring your drawings and descriptions to an intellectual property attorney and discuss whether it makes sense to seek some kind of protection. Plus, before you invest too much time and energy in your product, it's a good idea to do an intellectual property search to make sure nobody else has already created what you want to create and protected the right to sell it.

Depending on your concept, you might want to explore whether you can create the first version of it yourself. The more you can do, the better. It'll save you money down the road. Yogitoes founder, Susan Nichols, tried creating her Skidless yoga mat cover from a wide variety of readily available fabrics and products before seeking outside help.

If you can't create your product prototype yourself, you'll want to find a professional prototyper to do it for you. Yes, there are actually people and companies that specialize in this. Just Google "prototyper" to find resources, look at their areas of specialty, portfolios, and always ask for references and meet with several before committing to any. You may not need a professional prototyper. For example, if your product is something that could be sewn, a local tailor or seamstress might be able to do it for you for a reasonable price.

Prototypers will generally meet with you for a free initial consultation, give you an estimate based on an hourly rate (usually between $75 and $150 an hour), and, if it's a fit, they'll ask for a deposit (generally 50 percent), commit to a fixed delivery date, and get to work. Once you've found a prototyper, you'll also want them to sign a nondisclosure agreement, or NDA, that helps to ensure they will not reveal the nature of your product to anyone else. You can have your attorney draft an NDA or search "NDA" to find samples. One drafted for your specific needs is best.

When you get your prototype, you can begin to test-market it, starting with those who are most likely to buy and resell your product. Get feedback, make any changes that make sense, and if needed have a revised prototype created.

When you are confident you have a product that is ready for market, it's time to make a big decision—manufacture or license.

If you want to keep control and make more money, manufacturing is generally the better option. But you'll also have to be willing to take on the burden of warehousing, fulfillment, sales, marketing, insurance, and customer service, which can be a real hassle. You'll be running a full-time business, selling your wares, going to trade shows, and more. If you're truly passionate about what you're creating, this can be exciting and energizing. I tend to be that person. But a lot of people are more interested in creating a product, then stepping back and letting someone else run with it.

If the work and responsibility of manufacturing and selling your product yourself doesn't sound like so much fun, you may be able to license the right to manufacture and sell your product to another person or company in exchange for a royalty, generally a percentage of revenue. Also, the manufacturing option may require you to place a minimum order, often thousands of items. If you don't have access to the funds needed to manufacture your product, licensing may be your salvation.

You'll still need to do the early development work, but eventually, you will be able to essentially hand your product over to someone else to run with. You make less money, but the work is theirs. Plus, if you find the right licensing partner, one with good resources, connections, and distribution partners, they may be able to bring your product to market in a way you never could. You'll earn less per item, but benefit from substantially higher sales.

A word of warning: there are a lot of scammers in the world of inventions, so be very careful about working with invention submission and promotion firms, especially ones that require you to pay to have a relationship with them. Research firms thoroughly, check them out online, with the Better Business Bureau, and your state's attorney general's office. Do your homework, so you don't end up getting burned.

Here are some resources to get you going with product prototyping, manufacturing, and licensing.

Prototyping

- InventorsAlliance.org. Inventor's Alliance is an organization designed to help educate inventors who seek to sell their ideas.
- Inventorspot.com. This website features a wealth of articles on inventing, manufacturing, licensing, and distribution. It includes many links to nearly every resource you'll need, including prototypers, manufacturers, designers, lawyers, service providers, and other outside resources.
- InventRight.com. This is a blog, educational resource, and mixed-media program created by well-known inventor Steven Keys that teaches a soup-to-nuts approach

to product development and licensing. It is about the most comprehensive resource I've seen for product licensing.

- United Inventor's Association (www.UIAUSA.org). This is the website for the UIA, an organization that supports inventors and product developers.

Manufacturing

- Thomasnet.com. This is a directory of manufacturers, searchable by specialty.
- Macraesbluebook.com. This is another major directory of manufacturers, searchable by specialty.

Books

- *The Mom Inventors Handbook: How to Turn Your Great Idea into the Next Big Thing* by Tamara Monosoff (McGraw-Hill, 2005).
- *How to License Your Million Dollar Idea: Everything You Need to Know to Turn a Simple Idea into a Million Dollar Payday,* 2nd ed. by Harvey Reese (Wiley, 2002).
- *The Inventor's Bible: How to License and Market Your Brilliant Ideas* by Ronald Louis Docie (Ten Speed Press, 2004).

EIGHT

Exploit the Need for Community

IT'S NOT UNUSUAL FOR A vibrant community to develop around a pursuit. We often draw as much enjoyment from our involvement in that community as we do from our participation in the core activity, because, by nature, we thrive around like-minded people.

The pervasive need to interact with like-minded people is a driving force behind the growth of some of the largest online social networks, like Facebook.com and MySpace .com.

Communities generally form in a somewhat organic manner around activities. But sometimes communities need a bit of help coming together. They need someone to play the role of community catalyst or creator. Therein lies yet another opportunity to satisfy your passion and make money along the way.

Build an Online Community and Turn It into Income

When blogs first hit the online world, they were largely vehicles for writers to share what was on their minds. Readers could respond, but they'd have to do it through e-mail or instant messaging. All that changed however, when the major blogging platforms added the ability for readers to add their own comments. This single change was instrumental in turning blogs from bully pulpits into places for serious conversation. Indeed, blogs have become about the most powerful vehicle for building a worldwide community online, which makes them near-perfect vehicles for building communities around passions.

Liz's Story
Tavern Keeper's Daughter Brings Banter Online

Liz Strauss, founder of Successful-Blog.com is, perhaps, the ultimate example of bringing a community together online. The daughter of a tavern owner, Liz grew up in a culture reminiscent of the Cheers bar.

To her, life is about conversation; it's what makes her come alive. So, it's not surprising that she runs her blog the way someone else might run their bar.

Ostensibly built around the topic of blogging, Successful-Blog.com has evolved into a worldwide conversation about life.

A perfect example is Liz's online open-mic nights.

Every Tuesday, Liz posts a question on her blog, then turns her comment section into a free-for-all. Readers begin by sharing their thoughts on the initial question, then often veer off onto side topics, discussions among themselves, and at times mildly controlled chaos. The conversations sometimes go on for days and it's not unusual for a single three-hundred-word post to end up with two to three hundred comments, before the conversation moves on.

Why would people hang out at Liz's blog, as opposed to Facebook, MySpace, or some other virtual social gathering place? Same reason people go to the local pub or quilting club at a friend's home. Sometimes you'd just rather be with a small group of friends that keep coming back every week than find your way through a sea of seventy million online revelers.

Interestingly, Liz does very little advertising on Successful-Blog.com. For the first few years, her main approach to making money from, or monetizing, her community was to leverage the way the blog positioned her as an expert on online community building and turn that expertise into consulting fees. Now, she's taken the next step, serving her ferociously loyal community's desire to learn and interact in person with the *creation of her annual SOBCon (Successful and Outstanding Bloggers Conference) blogging business conference that lures people to Chicago for an annual blogging conference.*

Build a High-Value Peer Network

Where Liz and many other bloggers satisfy their jones to interact with others around a focused pursuit online, oftentimes similar opportunities exist all around us in the offline world. So, if you have a passion to connect with people and a second passion for a specific activity or interest, explore whether there is a need for a more coherent community to support your interest. If so, creating that community can be a great source of passion-satisfaction and income.

Victoria's Story
Former Lawyer and Dot-Commer Turns Professional Connector

Ladies Who Launch cofounder Victoria Colligan followed this very path. For her, that sense of passion came from pursuing the process of entrepreneurship and engaging in conversations and building relationships with other women.

She was a natural connector and loved to bring people together, especially women who were on a mission. Victoria also loved the process of building and creating. To paraphrase Lifehacker's Gina Trapani, these were the activities and processes she "couldn't not do."

So, after a short stint in law, followed by a slightly longer one in business development during the dot-com boom, Colligan began to get the urge to turn her passion for connecting and building into her living.

The nice thing about having a passion for connecting is that there are, in fact, many ways to generate a significant living from it. Her experience in business revealed an information and connection gap. There was no national organization devoted to nurturing entrepreneurship among women with a strong on- and offline presence.

This revelation inspired Victoria to blend her passion to connect with and inspire women with the culture of entrepreneurship in a quest to fill the gap and earn a living. So, she teamed with partner Beth Schoenfeldt to found Ladies Who Launch (LWL). LWL is a national organization that brings together women entrepreneurs and provides a wide range of education and support, including a website packed with information (www.ladieswholaunch.com), resources and profiles, local chapters that provide regular opportunities to network, learn, and partner (called incubators), and a schedule of live events and conferences.

In a remarkably short time, Colligan and Schoenfeldt's company grew to boast hundreds of thousands of members.

Build Upon What You Know

Liz Strauss and Victoria Colligan are both great examples of people who, in very different ways, created a comfortable living by building and guiding a community around a specific activity or content area.

Liz's initial vehicle for bringing people together was a blog. Her strategy to make money was to leverage her proven ability to build a hugely interactive community and the notoriety that it provided into consulting jobs teaching others how to do the same. And, that eventually led to additional revenue as a conference organizer.

Victoria and Beth also began with a strong online effort, but rather than a traditional blog, they built a more extensive, feature-laden, case-study, and forum-driven website and launched a network of local live incubators, events, and conferences, earning fees for each. Their growing platform led to a book in 2007, *Ladies Who Launch,* that added not only revenue, but national branding and awareness.

The critical rule in exploring community building as a path to passion and prosperity is, first and foremost, make sure you have a deep enough love of the core activity or content area. Creating, growing, and leading a community requires a lot of work. Passion is what will keep you going, especially in the early days. Plus, because people respond powerfully to energy and authenticity, possessing these qualities will be key to effectively rallying people to your shared cause.

Then, the big question is how to turn community into income.

The vehicles and approaches are endless. They range from blog or online forum-driven revenue to local clubs or organizational meetings, paid events, conferences, teleseminars, webinars, retreats, speaking, consulting, corporate sponsorships, and beyond.

Plus, from a marketing standpoint, a well-nourished community is also a trusting, hungry market. So, you might explore blending career renegade paths and combining your passion for community with an interest in educating the group, producing premium content, guides, books, kits, DVDs, or other paid content. We've seen this approach in the earlier examples of bloggers building large communities, developing a strong understanding of their needs, then selling information and education products into those communities.

Once you've rallied the community, your options are many. Your biggest challenge will likely become not how to generate income from the community, but how to do it in a way that is respectful and continually fuels your passion for both the people and the pursuit. And that's a good challenge to have.

NINE

Make It Easier for People to Do What You Love

SOMETIMES, YOU'LL FIND GAPS IN actual services or products offered in your sphere of passion. But what if the service or product you'd love to provide is already being offered? Time to go one layer deeper and ask a few questions that often reveal one of the sneakiest passion gaps available.

- Are there any gaps in the *way* the service or product is being offered, sold, or delivered?
- Are there people or places who would benefit from better or easier access to this or a similar service or product?

Apple's iPod is a great example of this. Music has been around for as long as we have, and it was available in digital format for years before the iPod hit the scene. But that little device profoundly changed the *way* the music was delivered and its sister program, iTunes, provided easy access to instantly downloadable music. The revolution wasn't about bigger and better content, it was about bigger and better access. Apple wasn't selling music, they were selling cool and ease.

Sometimes mode gaps exist in the way a product or service is delivered. Other times, it can exist in the form of geographic limitations.

When my yoga studio, Sonic Yoga, launched in November 2001, there was already great yoga in New York. But, outside of New York, L.A., San Francisco, and a handful of other major cities, the rest of the country was seriously behind the curve. And, I knew it would be a long time before enough teachers were trained and deployed through the country to bring a high-quality experience to a mass market. I also knew that the yoga we taught was very physical and dynamic and was a tremendous tool for fitness and weight loss.

Previous research and business experience in the mainstream fitness world demonstrated a consistently high demand for weight loss and fitness solutions, and research into yoga participation and media-product sales indicated that demand for yoga was growing rapidly on a national level.

It seems I'd discovered an access gap that could be exploited on a national level by commoditizing and distributing New York–style yoga. The best way to tap this market was to commoditize the live New York City teaching experience by translating that experience to video and making the videos available to a mass market.

Plus, as an added benefit, I knew having our own videos would be a big reputation booster and help drive revenue during our first year in business.

I didn't want to spend much money to create my educational exploit, though, so I decided to handle the entire project in-house. I went online and researched the process of video production, editing, mastering, replication, packaging, and distribution. We used the studio as our set, tapped our regular class students to be the students in the video, and e-mailed everyone we knew to find people with cameras and access to editing equipment.

I then began calling around to small, local record labels, who had music I thought might work well on the video. I found one that was willing to take a risk on us and license their music for 100 percent back end and a mention in the credits. We paid nothing up front, but gave them a royalty on each sale and displayed their website at the end. One of our student's boyfriends was an editor and indy filmmaker, so we paid him a day fee and a back end royalty, too.

Once the filming and editing was done, I found a company online that copied and packaged the videos for a very reasonable fee, although we had to order 2,500 units to get a good price (we literally stocked those in a massage room at the studio, which soon turned into our shipping headquarters).

A few months earlier, I'd pulled off a pretty unusual marketing and PR coup in connection with the video (see chapter 17), so the videos started flying off the shelves within days. That first printing quickly sold out and we went through a number of additional print runs, before finally outsourcing the order processing and fulfillment and redirecting all orders, via our website, to them.

Did we have our problems? Sure. Because we were pretty much making it up as we went. At one point, we were so backlogged, half the day was spent refunding orders and talking to customers all over the country who clearly desperately needed a yoga buzz. A few years later, with a fuller selection of videos and DVDs for sale, our fulfillment company went out of business, overnight, taking our entire inventory with them. But, we got through it and, in the end, the decision to fill the national yoga-access gap with DVDs was not only a huge moneymaker, but, also, a tremendous reputation builder. People were literally paying us to expand our brand.

TEN

Planning and Protecting Your Vision

WHAT ABOUT THINGS LIKE BUSINESS formats (corporations, LLCs, partnerships), insurance, copyrights, trademarks? What about business plans, spreadsheets, and all that other nitty-gritty business stuff?

Depending on what you are exploring, you may need some, all, or none of the above. These items start to dance dangerously close to providing legal advice, which I cannot do in the context of this book but would strongly encourage you to seek. Still, I want to say a few words about each.

Business Formats

At a certain point, you'll probably want to consider whether to do business as yourself or form what's called a business entity, like a corporation or limited liability company (LLC) to do business "on your behalf." Depending which you choose, there may be some very real tax and liability benefits to forming a business entity, the biggest one being, these entities can shield your personal assets should the business not work out. A great resource to learn more about the different entities, fees, and benefits is www.Incorporate.com, which provides a wealth of information about the basics of starting and structuring any new business, from choosing a name to writing a business plan.

Business Plans

Business plans play a major role in making sure you've considered all aspects of your adventure, fleshed out your concept, researched your market, competition, and costs, and projected your financial needs. They are all but required in traditional fund-raising. Once the plan has been created, it's a good idea to revise it on an ongoing basis, in an effort to keep it relevant and useful. Without updating, most business plans get stale very quickly. Even if you don't use the plan going forward (and many people don't), simply having done the work to complete it will arm you with information and answers that you'll find invaluable.

A word of caution about creating a business plan: Don't use it as an excuse to avoid getting started. Much of the exploration laid out in this book can be completed with little or no investment and without need of a business plan. Honestly, much of it can be completed, even going forward, with a very streamlined plan, because the paths focus largely on swapping time for money, thereby minimizing your risk. Here are some killer resources to learn more about when and why to write a plan and how best to do it.

- How to write a business plan: ten questions with Tim Berry (http:// blog.guykawasaki.com/2007/07/how-to-write-a- .html). Venture capitalist, entrepreneurship author, and blogger Guy Kawasaki offers a revealing interview with leading business plan software creator, Tim Berry, who shares great advice about what's really important in creating a business plan.
- BPlans.com. Offers Business Plan Pro software, an industry-leading program that walks you step-by-step through the process of creating your business plan. The site also includes a vast library of free articles on planning and operating a wide variety of off- and online business, along with tools, calculators, and more

than one hundred free samples of completed business plans.

- SBA.gov. This website is home to the Small Business Administration and provides a wealth of information and free tools, resources, and spreadsheets for all aspects of starting and running a small business.
- Going without a plan in the tech-world (http://blog.guy kawasaki.com/2007/06/no-plan-no-capi.html). Finally, circling back to Guy Kawasaki for a contrarian point of view on business planning, this post features video presentation of a panel Guy led called, "No Plan, No Capital, No Model . . . No Problem." It boasts a roundup of tech-entrepreneurs who've collectively made a bundle wearing their pajamas, often working part time and never even considering creating a business plan.

Intellectual Property

The more innovative your idea, the more important it is to protect it from being copied. The type of protection you'll want to explore will vary depending on the nature of what you are doing. As a general rule, patents protect inventions, copyrights protect literary and artistic works, and trade/service-marks protect visual expressions of ideas, services, products, or brands. When artist Ann Rea decided to reproduce her artwork on merchandise and considered licensing it for wine bottles, she bought a book on intellectual property. Now, there are great websites that help you understand what is protectable, when, and how. Here, again, your best bet it to seek out the expertise of an intellectual property attorney. To get you started, you can gather a tremendous amount of information at USPTO.gov, the website for the United States Patent and Trademark Office. The USPTO is the agency that regulates intellectual property in the United States. You learn about the different types of intellectual property rights, search to see if anyone else has already filed for protection for a similar word, invention, or mark and even file an application online. Also, for the most accurate information, this search must be supplemented by a more detailed search conducted by an attorney or service agency.

ELEVEN

Is the World Ready for You?

PASSION IS ESSENTIAL, BUT YOU'LL also need a hungry market with deep enough pockets. Ignore its absence at your peril. Harness it, bundle it with passion, access it with permission, and you're in business.

Before you invest your heart, soul, and, potentially, money, you need to ask a single, critical question: *Are there enough people who desire the products or services created by the pursuit of my passion who are willing to pay enough for it to allow me to live comfortably in the world?*

Because, if the answer is no, then it's game over. Your idea needs to be tweaked, changed, or abandoned. It doesn't matter how much *you* love something if nobody else likes it enough to pay for it or to pay you to do it. You may be crazy about bacon-flavored pudding, but if everyone else feels the way I do about it—that it's a revolting idea—you'll never be able to sell it. So how do you find out if anyone will pay for what makes you come alive?

Start with Intuition and Observation

First, draw upon your personal experience. Look at the activities you love to do and ask what's missing. Sometimes the answer is right in front of you. Other times you need to dig deeper and brainstorm to discover, then validate, an opportunity.

Susan Nichols drew upon her own frustration, slipping on sweaty yoga mats, then confirmed her hunch through conversations with friends in the local community. The information she gathered gave her the confidence to take the next steps. It took a whole lot more creativity, though, for Ann Rea to uncover an opportunity painting and selling renderings of vineyards to high-income tourists while they visited wine country. She crossed a lot of options off her list before following that one.

Start by refining your idea and assessing demand from your own experience and intuition. But don't stop there, because doing so leads to one of the biggest mistakes you can make in exploring market demand—the assumption that your likes and dislikes accurately reflect those of your market. You may, in fact, be that rare person with her finger on the pulse of the market's secret heartbeat, but your hunch may also be anywhere from slightly to totally off.

Begin to expand your sphere of inquiry to friends, family, and anyone else who shares your passion in an effort to help you find or create renegade opportunities. Share your ideas and ask what they think about their feasibility.

Realize, though, opinions of friends and family are likely still not enough, because they are laced with subjective opinion and personal expectations. Those closest to you are often quick to support you and slow to criticize. Or, they might take the opposite approach, condemning ideas without a valid reason.

So, before you dive in and follow your passion into a major change in direction, or invest time and money into a model, prototype, demo, or full-blown business, do a bit more legwork. It will pay off in the long run. Gather information so you can decide whether to take action, modify your path, or put this path to bed and pursue another.

Start Broad, then Drill Down

Beyond intuition, personal experience, observation, and personal conversations, how do you find out if there is a hungry market? Big companies and marketing firms rely on all sorts of techniques to research markets, from focus groups to industry surveys to fMRI's of the brain, none of which come cheap.

I've spent money on various forms of market research, but, over the years, I've found a number of highly useful, renegade tools and techniques that deliver a ton of information either for free or for very little money. I'll share these below.

As you do the research to discover whether a hungry enough market exists, start with the broadest possible description of the customers, the solution, and the needs you want to address, then narrow the descriptions and questions.

For example, when Ann Rea decided to pursue a career as an artist, she began with the entire field of painting. She made a list of every conceivable way to make money painting, then began to research each item on that list. As she learned more, she ruled out options until she finally found a market that jumped out at her, the one she pursued.

The tools and techniques below are presented in order of *relative scope*. The ones closer to the top are best for gathering information about broader markets and areas of interest, while the ones further down will be increasingly effective at providing market information about specific products, ideas, or services.

Try to define exactly what it is that you would like to

do and narrow the scope of your inquiry as much as possible *before* you take your research online. This will lessen the volume of information you find, decrease the likelihood of irrelevant information, and just make the process more manageable. The last thing you want to do is set yourself up to be overwhelmed.

Online Searches

The first place nearly everyone goes to learn about anything these days is Google. It's a great place to start. Step one is to brainstorm the major keywords and phrases. See who else is doing what you're doing, how much is written about it, and what comes up on the first few pages. This should give you some nice background.

We are going to learn how to jack-up Google searches with a handful of other free tools and browser plug-ins to reveal far more market information than a standard Google search.

Find the Major Keywords that People Use to Search for More Information About Your Interest, Hobby, or Passion

Start with the ones you would use. Then, go to: http://tools.seobook.com/keyword-tools/seobook/. There you will find the keyword research tool from SEOBook.com, with a place to enter keywords. Let's try it out. Enter one of the keywords or phrases from your list, then click the submit button.

Within a few seconds the page will refresh and you will see something amazing. Down the left side of the page will be your keyword or phrase along with a list of related keywords or phrases. They are listed in order of search volume. The next few columns will list the estimated number of times each keyword or phrase has been searched on Google .com, Yahoo.com, MSN.com, and Wordtracker.com, then provide an estimated overall daily search volume. This is tremendously useful in gauging interest in your hobby or passion. Look for keywords that are most relevant and see how many other people are looking for information about those keywords every day.

When I searched using the word "yoga" SEOBook revealed that the keyword phrase with the top search volume was "nude yoga," with an estimated 13,481 searches a day. Interestingly, the word "yoga" only had 5,199 searches. Go figure. Multiply 13,481 by thirty days in the month and you get 404,430 searches a month for nude yoga. So, if I were looking to somehow make money in the yoga services world, guess where I might focus my energy? Okay, let's not actually go there, but you get the point. Try this a few days in a row to make sure this wasn't a random spike.

Now, let's say I had another hobby I'd also be interested in making some money from. Clogging. So, I plug the word "clogging" into the SEOBook.com search tool and I learn the top search term is "clogging shoes." But, I am much more interested in the act of clogging and teaching it. The second most searched-on term is "clogging," which was searched for a grand total of 3,390 times across all search engines all over the world in the last month.

Does that sound like enough interest to make it worth pursuing? Probably not. Unless it happens to be a low-volume, yet high-ticket item that can generate significant income with few sales or it's a service or commodity with a slim online community or presence. That's where intuition and personal experience always serve to gut check statistics and research.

Localize and Verify Longer-Term Trends with Google Trends

Some interests, hobbies, or passions can be turned into sources of income without regard to geographic location. Others, though, require a sizable local market. Activities that require face-to-face contact, such as personal services, are perfect examples. If your passion falls into this category, you need a way to uncover where the online searches are coming from or, more accurately, whether they are coming from your area.

At the same time, you want to see if the information you discovered in the step above was just a blip on the radar, an anomaly, or part of a legitimate longer-term trend.

One tool to satisfy both questions is a service called Google Trends that allows you to see:

- A graph that shows the search trend for your keywords, letting you know whether the trend is up, down, or sideways
- The top ten countries, regions (states), and cities the searches are coming from
- Major related news stories that correlate with any major moves of spikes on the trend graph
- The languages being used to search

To use Google Trends, you can either visit www.Google .com/trends, then type in your chosen keywords or click on your keywords under the Google Trends column in the SEOBook keyword search tool. When I did a Google Trends search on nude yoga, the greatest number of searches, worldwide, came from Utah—who knew? You can also add multiple search terms in the search field on top and get comparative graphs.

Use SEOBook.com Search Tools

Who's talking about your topic? On your SEOBook Search Tools results page, scroll down past the search results and you will see a second section. This area provides an abundance of links to tools, websites, news sources, conversation hubs, search engines, and blogs that allow you to learn more about who's searching for your passion, what they're talking about, and where they are. Take the time to explore them. Start to look for consensus. Gather as much information as possible from those websites and blogs about the activities, the markets, who is already serving those markets, whether anyone else is doing what you are thinking about doing, whether they are succeeding and where.

Search by Topic with Clusty.com

Clusty.com is a great addition to your online searching and market research. Similar to Google, it allows you to type in any keywords or phrases, but, rather than kicking back a list of pages that could leave you searching for days, it adds a menu on the left side that clusters the top results by topic. This feature allows you to immediately rule out entire groups of websites that are only tangentially related or completely unrelated to what you were searching for.

For example, I searched on the phrase "yoga mats that do

not slip" and Clusty.com delivered a long list of results. First came the standard sponsored results, followed by organic search results in the main area. Then, on the left, were the top 181 results clustered by topic. The top ten topics are displayed, but you can click on the "all clusters" link immediately below those to see the full list.

From the topic list, we can immediately rule out whole categories of results as off-topic and hone in on others; this is a great time-saver. You can also search for more specific information within the clusters of topics, using the "find in clusters" search field underneath the topic list.

Use Mozilla's Firefox Browser to Surf the Web

Firefox allows you to install certain extra programs called add-ons that give you critical information about a website's popularity. You can download and install Firefox at http://www.mozilla.com.

From the Mozilla home page, click on the Add-Ons menu item, then, when the add-on page opens, search for the "Alexa" add-on. This will take you to a page with a list of add-ons. Look for the Alexa Sparky add-on (it may have a version number, that's fine). Click on the "Add to Firefox" button, then follow the instructions to install the Alexa add-on in your Firefox Web browser.

Read the terms of service. Alexa will collect information about your Web browsing as long as it is installed. So, make sure you are okay with this. We'll be tapping that very information and using it for our market research. If you are concerned about your personal privacy, then only use Firefox with Alexa for market research or just uninstall the Alexa add-on once you are done.

The browser will restart, then you'll notice two new items on the bottom right side of the browser window that will look like a line graph next to a number.

The line graph represents the overall traffic trends for whatever website is open in the browser window since 2004. And, the blue bar and number to the right provide the current Alexa rank, which give a numerical indication of how well trafficked that same website has been for the last three months. The closer to one, the more popular the website. For example, Yahoo! is number one. Any number under one hundred thousand shows a decent amount of traffic. An Alexa rank that is more than one million reveals very little traffic to any given site. Now your browser is ready for our renegade market research.

Using Firefox with the Alexa add-on, do a Google search on the most relevant and popular terms you discovered using SEOBook.com and Google Trends. Let's stay with the nude yoga example.

When I type this keyword phrase in, I get a search results page. This page gives us a ton of useful information. It gives us the organic search results in the main section. We'll come back to this, but let's look at some of the subtler information.

There is a blue horizontal bar toward the top of the page that separates the search box from the results below. To the right side of that bar, we see that there are 603,000 webpages that reference nude yoga. Wow, that sounds like a lot of people are writing about naked yoga! Then we take a look at the right side of the page. That's where people and companies pay to have their advertisements appear whenever certain keywords or phrases are searched on. Normally there are pages and pages of ads. The more you pay, the higher up your ad appears.

When I search on nude yoga, though, I notice something interesting about the ads. I scroll a few more pages to confirm my observation. They are almost entirely about sex, not legit nude yoga. Not exactly on point. It appears that nobody is actually advertising nude yoga classes on Google.com.

You might be ready to yell, "Eureka!," but this is actually a bad thing. You *want* to be in a market where people are already advertising, preferably on a consistent, long-term basis. This is what's called proof of demand. If there is a market for something, there will always be people lining up to advertise to that market. So the lack of advertisers strongly suggests a lack of a viable market. People either tried to advertise and determined it wasn't worth the effort or nobody has begun to tap that market yet.

Could you be the person to create a new market or solution? Yes, but the educational burden to instill broad awareness of a problem and demonstrate how what you do solves that problem is often massive. The work it takes to create a new market is far beyond what most people are ready or willing to handle.

When I look back at the search results on the main part of the page, the first two listings are spammy voyeuristic websites. The third is a place I recognize as offering naked yoga classes in NYC (no, I've never been, but I'm in the biz, so I have to stay abreast of certain things). That listing is a review in a large magazine website, though, so it's not going to get me what I want. I am trying to get to the source, the service, and product providers.

So I scroll down a few more and find a listing for nude yoga studios in other major cities. I click on it and here is where the Alexa add-on comes into play. Once on the page, I look at the Alexa rank. I see it is 2,360,000. That tells me that this website gets very little traffic. I do this for another studio devoted to nude yoga in another major city and find an Alexa rank of 3,279,293. Even worse than the first. I click on a third and the results continue to back up the trend. Not strong support for demand for nude yoga. People may be searching for nude yoga, but they're not clicking on the websites that show an interest in what I am thinking about offering. Indeed, the pages and pages of erotic-yoga advertisers tell me a good chunk of the search traffic is looking for something more sexually oriented. Those ads wouldn't be there if they weren't making money.

At this point, I've gathered a lot of information about people searching for this thing I love to do and am thinking about turning into a source of revenue. And, while the Google ads suggest a DVD of naked erotic yoga might indeed have a market, that's not where my interests lie.

Interestingly, at my first Career Renegade Bootcamp, I did this exercise live with a professional organizer, who was struggling to define and grow the business. We were all blown away to learn that nearly all of the organic search results and advertisements had terrible Alexa ranks, suggesting (a) it's a tough business with a limited market, (b) it's one of those highly localized businesses that does not rely strongly on the Internet as a source of marketing or information-dissemination, or (c) it's a business where people can survive with little traffic and a small number of clients who pay a lot of money. Again, this is where your own knowledge, experience, observations, and your background research will help determine what is really going on. You'll want to take these factors into consideration in your exploration, too.

You can gather a tremendous amount of information

through these turbocharged search techniques and tools. This should be your starting place, but there are still a handful of other renegade tools and techniques that will help you figure out whether there are enough people interested in what you are considering turning into a source of money to put in the effort.

Do a ClickBank Search

Anytime there is a demand for a product or service, there will also generally be a demand for information about that product or service. This leads people to create information products, like e-books, that can be downloaded. One of the biggest ways to promote these products is to register as a merchant at a website called ClickBank.com, then describe your product and offer a commission or "affiliate fee" to anyone who promotes or advertises your product and leads to a sale.

The affiliate side of ClickBank.com allows potential affiliates to search on all the different info-products being offered and see statistics on how in demand the various products are. As career renegades, we can mine this information as a source of free information for market research by searching the interests, hobbies, or passions we are interested in turning into revenue sources; seeing what information products are being sold around those interests; and noting the relative demand for each. A lot of products with a lot of demand is a good sign. It means people are hungry enough for information about our passion to pay for it.

To do this:

- Go to www.ClickBank.com, click on the "promote products" tab on the top of the page, then click on the "marketplace" tab. This will take you to a page with a form that allows you to search by category, subcategory, product-type, keyword, language, and popularity.

- Enter the category, keywords, or product type that best represents what you are thinking about doing.

- You'll be taken to a results page with a listing of similar products, along with stats that reveal the price, popularity, and commission being paid to promote each item.

- Scroll through the first fifty items and see if any are close to what you are considering. If there are few items, that may be a sign of lack of demand. If there are many items, this reveals higher market demand, but also more competition.

- Click on the "view pitch page" link to see what price the product is selling at. Then, on the ClickBank results page, for the same listing look at "total $/sale" amount to see how much commission the merchant is paying for each sale. I found a set of DVDs that teach guitar for $39.95 and paid a $26 commission, leaving $13.95 in net profit. This gives you a feel for the price levels of similar solutions and what you'll be left with after promotional expenses.

- Then look at the "gravity" number. This gives you a feel for how many sales have taken place over the last eight weeks.

Together, this information adds to your understanding of market demand and also gives you a sense for pricing and promotional expense.

Magazines, Newspapers, Newsletters, Blogs, and Websites

Visit your local bookstore or magazine stand and see what magazines or newspapers serve people with your interest, hobby, or passion. The more, the better. Then, take a look through each. How big are they? Only a few pages, less than one hundred, or hundreds of pages? The more pages, the better, because it shows a level of interest in information about your passion and the existence of a community around it.

Assess the level of advertisers. Are they local, regional, national, or international? Are the ads full-color? What percentage of total pages are taken up with ads that are a quarter page or more? Big, beautiful ads cost a lot of money, so a publication with plentiful ads is a sign of strong demand and a willingness of participants to spend money.

If there are more than five or ten national or local magazines, newspapers, or newsletters serving your niche, that's a good sign. If at least 30 percent of the total pages are filled with ads and at least half of those sport more expensive quarter-page or larger ads, that's a great sign too. People don't pay to print big, full-color magazines or run display-ads unless they are making a positive return on their money (at least they won't do either for long at a loss).

Then, turn to websites and blogs and look for the same thing. How many established blogs or websites serve your niche? How much traffic do they have (look at the Alexa rank). What is the average number of comments on each of the last thirty posts? Fewer than five suggests a small community.

Do they serve ads? Who are the advertisers? Take the time to search on all the different keywords related to your passion, then add in the words "business," "income," "career," "trend" and gather as much information as possible from public discussion, articles, and reports.

The volume of print publications and ads are more compelling proof of market viability than online publications and ads because the fixed costs of putting out a print publication generally far exceed those associated with an online analogue. There's a lot more on the line, so seeing established print publications with a lot of larger ads that serve your niche tells you someone's making enough money to pay the cost of printing and advertising.

Mine Craigslist to Find Local Interest

If what you would like to do is constrained by location or you'd prefer to test the waters locally when first starting out, you may also want to spend some time on Craigslist .com, the Internet's home for classifieds. Craigslist continues to expand to include nearly every major market in the world and the vast majority of ads are free.

Once at Craigslist.com, select your region, if available, or if it's not available, find the closest region or region with a similar demographic to yours. Then select the category from the main part of the page where your activity is most likely to be listed or just search for specific keywords, using the search field on the left. You will then be shown a list of headlines for classified ads posted over the last seven days, some of which will be quite long, that included your keywords or phrases. Click on the ads that are relevant and examine them. How relevant are the ads to what you want to do? And what prices are people charging? Scroll back through the entire one-week listing period. Do this for a few weeks to see if the ads you have noted are repeated.

Seeing ads repeated on Craigslist is an indicator of the existence of market interest, though it's a fairly weak one. It's not nearly as strong an indicator as repeated paid advertisements would be, because with free classifieds the investment is zero, so even if the ads weren't working, there's no downside to repeatedly posting them.

Find Out What's Hot on eBay

We all know eBay as the world's biggest online auction. But, eBay also publishes a monthly hot-items list that shows what general categories and specific items are in most demand on eBay.

Generally speaking, merchandise that is hot on eBay will also be in great demand in most any retail setting. The hot-items list, though, is not very helpful in sussing out demand for services or products that don't translate well to an online or auction selling format.

You can find the monthly hot-items list, along with a bunch of useful market information at http://pages.ebay .com/sellercentral/catalog.html.

In the seller's area, eBay also publishes category tips that look at the major categories of merchandise selling on eBay and share information about trends and techniques in each category. You can find that information at http://pages .ebay.com/sellercentral/sellbycategory.html.

Set Up a Pay-Per-Click Ad Trial

The above renegade tools and techniques give you a feel for the existence of a general demand and size of the market for what you want to offer. But, especially if you are exploring tapping your passion through entrepreneurship, before you invest time and money, you'll want more detailed information.

You'll want to know if there is a hungry enough market for the specific product or service you want to offer.

This next step will cost you a bit of money, but, within hours or days it will go a long way toward either confirming the existence of a market and begin to build a prospect list or revealing a lack of interest that could save you a lot of wasted time, energy, and money.

It will help:

- Identify demand for the very specific service or product you want to offer
- Give a feel for the bigger market demand

- Allow you to begin to hone in on local market demand
- Build a list of prospective customers

There are two steps:

- Set up a pay-per-click or free online advertising campaign
- Set up a one-page lead-generation website

Let's go through each step.

Step 1. Post Pay-Per-Click or Free Online Ads

Remember when we looked at those small text ads on the right side of the Google search results page? Those are called pay-per-click (PPC) ads, because the advertisers only pay when someone clicks on the link in an ad. So, if you were a PPC advertiser, your ad could be shown a thousand times, but you would only pay when someone clicked on it.

PPC ads can be found on Google.com, MSN.com, Yahoo.com, and a wide variety of other ad services. You can sign up for advertising accounts with each for free, then enter your advertising text, choose the keywords you would like the ad to be linked to, the amount you are willing to pay for each click, and set a daily or monthly expense cap.

PPC ads are most often displayed on the search results pages when keywords relevant to those ads are searched upon. Depending on the service, they may also be displayed on a combination of websites and blogs with content that matches keywords chosen by the advertiser. Certain services even allow advertisers to limit the ads to certain geographic regions or zones.

Here are links to pages in each major service that help guide you through their processes:

- Adwords.Google.com
- Searchmarketing.Yahoo.com
- Advertising.Microsoft.com

Even if you don't end up using each account, I would still suggest signing up for all three, because as an advertiser you will get free access to their keyword search tools. These will let you enter all the keywords you've been exploring, provide more detailed information about search volume and suggested additional or alternative keywords, and competition for each keyword.

You can start with a very modest budget. Very often $100 to $200 will get you enough information to know whether there is a market hungry enough to put more serious energy into the effort. Just be sure to bid enough to ensure your ad appears on the first page of search results, preferably in the top five ads. The different PPC ad services will estimate your ad placement, then let you adjust your bids to improve positioning.

The science and art of creating an effective Google Adwords campaign is far beyond the scope of this book. A great, easy-to-follow resource for a detailed, step-by-step approach to writing the most effective possible PPC ads, choosing bid levels, and getting the best response possible is Perry Marshall's *Ultimate Guide to Google Adwords.* Use Marshall's book as your guide.

Step 2. Post a One-Page Website

Of course, if you are going to place online ads, you also need to have a webpage to send people to when they click on the links in the ads.

First, go to GoDaddy.com, where you can choose a website address or URL, reserve it, then sign up for a free hosting account. This should cost around $10.

Once you've decided to move forward with your concept, you'll likely want to spend more time creating a compelling website. For our purposes, though, a simple, one-page website with a clean design will do.

If you know html (the programming language used to build basic webpages), you can create it and post it yourself. If not, go to elance.com, an online clearinghouse for freelance work, where you can post a request to have a one-page website built and receive responses in no time. It shouldn't cost more than about $50 to $100.

On your webpage, include basic information about your idea, with bullet points that describe the problem your idea will solve and as many benefits as you can think of. Again, should you choose to move forward with your idea, you will want to enhance this page, but for now, we are simply using it to gauge interest.

On my early one-page website that I used to launch my first Renegade Bootcamp, I had a form installed to capture the names and e-mail addresses of people who were interested. You can set this up at AWeber.com and have the person who creates your webpage include a similar form. This allows you to collect leads as you market test (and those leads may very well end up covering the cost of your PPC campaign).

Once your Google Adwords campaign goes live, your ads will be displayed on Google and other websites and people will begin to click on the ads, depleting your ad budget. After your account has been depleted, be sure to terminate the campaign, to ensure no more money is expended.

Then, log into your Adwords account, click on the campaign management tab, then click on the campaign summary subtab. Scroll down and you'll see your campaign stats, then look for the column with the heading CTR; this stands for click-thru rate. It shows the percentage of people who have clicked on the link in your ad versus the total number of times the ad was shown.

Providing you've done at least an average job of creating your Adwords advertisement (let Perry be your guide), your CTR will give you a reasonable idea of the level of interest in your idea. The higher your CTR, the more interest. And, if you include an e-mail form and offer something of value in exchange for a person's e-mail, you may very well end up with a list of prospects, too.

Run a Facebook Poll

With more than seventy million users, sixty-five billion page views a month, and the fastest growth in the over-twenty-five age range, Facebook.com is quickly becoming the world's social hub online. Most people set up a profile and use it as a home base to keep up with other friends through their Facebook profiles.

But what many people don't know is that Facebook boasts a growing number of professional and business applications too that can help provide inexpensive, lightning-fast market-demand information.

Facebook Polls allows you to set up online surveys that ask very specific questions to a designated number of Facebook members who match the demographics you choose. For example, you could ask eighteen- to twenty-five-year-old men in the New York area who were runners if they would be interested in a new product that would monitor their heart rates.

As I write this, it costs about 25 cents per person and you can get results in minutes, hours, or days. I would start with one hundred people and see what kind of answers you get before polling a larger group.

To set up your Facebook Poll, visit: http://www.face book.com/business/?polls.

Face-to-Face Investigation

While the above techniques leverage technology to allow you to acquire massive amounts of information in a very short period of time, you should still do a healthy amount of in-person exploration. Find out where the people you perceive to be your ultimate clients congregate, go there, and just ask questions. The basic questions would include:

- Are you experiencing the same problem as me?
- How strongly do you want a solution?

- Would you want to buy what I'd like to offer? How strongly?
- If not, could I change it to make it more desirable? How?
- Would you like something similar?
- Would you like something different?
- If so, what?
- What would you expect to pay?

The more detail you can bring to your renegade efforts, the better, more actionable information it is likely to yield.

A Word on Competition, Entrepreneurship, and Partnering

Your research may end up pointing you in any number of different directions. It might reveal enough interest to strengthen your desire to explore a particular path and take the next step. It may disclose a lack of interest and compel you to move on to something else. It may open up any number of related opportunities that you never even knew existed. Or, it may reveal a strong level of demand, but also a substantial amount of competition.

Competition is not a bad thing. It is a sign of demand. But if what you'd like to do is not different enough from someone else who is already serving your market, you generally have three options:

Go Head-to-Head with Them

This is only for the bold—and possibly the foolhardy. Trying to solve a problem or satisfy a need by doing the same thing your competitors are doing can be a fast track to failure. As long as demand outstrips supply, you're okay, but as soon as that equation begins to reverse (and it nearly always will) price wars begin, pain ensues, and someone's going down for the count.

Find a Way to Differentiate What You'd Like to Offer

Solve the problem in a different, better way. Dive deeper into the needs and desires of the people you'd like to serve and see if you can discover or create a different, preferably better way to bring your service or product to market and your passion to life.

If You Can't Beat 'Em, Join Them

Learn more about the people and companies who seem to already be doing what you'd love to do. Use the same tools and techniques to research them and find out if there might be an opportunity to join them. While many career renegades are entrepreneurs, starting a business is not a mandatory part of the equation. So, if you don't have the entrepreneurial bug or are not thrilled with the prospect of creating a business or profession that will allow you to cash in on your passion, see if those who are already doing it could use some help. For you, market research may lead to employment opportunities.

PART 3

How to Master Your
Passion and Build a
Worldwide Following

TWELVE

Are You Ready for the Renegade World?

WHEN I LAUNCHED A YOGA studio in the heart of
Manhattan with no formal training, no reputation, no following, and a ton of competition, a handful of the installed
yoga community was aghast. Who the hell was I to walk in,
set up shop, and just assume I had something to offer? Yet,
three hundred people packed the place in the first week,
and seven years later Sonic Yoga's been voted the number
one studio in NYC by Citysearch four times.

Some fields require a formal education, a mandatory
internship, or a license. Health care, law, and architecture
come to mind. If your passion lies in one of these pursuits,

then enduring more formalized education and licensing may be part of the cost of admission for you.

But, for an increasing number of career paths, demonstrable mastery and/or expert positioning regardless of pedigree are the keys to success. That may scare and anger a whole generation of people who came up under a different set of rules, but for career renegades, this phenomenon spells opportunity.

We'll get to ways to *demonstrate* your mastery, anoint yourself a public authority and open doors to cash in on your passion soon enough, but, for now, lets focus on *acquiring* the mastery that will allow you to turn passion into prosperity through renegade means.

Renegade Knowledge Acquisition Paths

What is the fastest, least expensive way to acquire the knowledge that will let you turn your passion into a source of income? The following knowledge acquisition paths are designed to position you to either dive directly into the path that makes you come alive or demonstrate your mastery in a manner that will open doors. The paths are listed in order, from easiest and most flexible to most challenging and formal.

If your primary goal is knowledge, the options toward

the top of the list will likely best satisfy your knowledge acquisition needs. For more formalized training or credentials, you'll likely land toward the bottom of the list.

Blogs, Podcasts, Websites, and Forums

It just doesn't get any easier than this. Increasingly, all the information you need is right there, in the public domain, twenty-four hours a day, for free. The market research tools and techniques you learned to explore opportunities will also likely reveal a wealth of information-packed online resources. Your job is simply to find the information resources and devote the time needed to immerse yourself in the quest for and mastery of knowledge.

Start with tools and techniques from chapter 4 to find websites and forums and read everything you can find. Then, check out Technorati.com and AllTop.com to find blogs and use iTunes or Audible.com to find relevant audio programs. You will be amazed how much is available for free! Some subject-area specific examples of great places to learn online include:

iTunes: Offers an extensive library of free educational podcasts. First, download the free iTunes software at http://www.apple.com/itunes/download/. Then, look at the left navigator bar, click "podcasts," then scroll halfway down the left side and click "education." The library grows larger every day.

Public video-sharing websites: The big video-aggregation websites are often great sources of information, especially how-to information that is better learned through visual demonstration. Websites to explore include:

YouTube.com

Video.google.com

Vimeo.com

Metacafe.com

WonderHowTo.com

VideoJug.com

ExpertVillage.com

Graspr.com

Subject-matter specific portals: Explore the leading blogs, websites, education portals, and resource pages that share information about the area you'd like to pursue. Great examples of blogs and websites with tremendous educational content include:

- PSDTuts.com. This blog offers an extensive library of Photoshop tutorials for those who are interested in not only learning the basics but the secrets of the pros.

- W3Schools.com. This website offers an extensive library of free tools, tips, and even full courses on website design and building. It has useful information for everyone from absolute beginners up through experienced developers.

- Digital-Photography-School.com. Offers in-depth instruction on digital photography, product reviews, and forums to facilitate interaction between members.

- ProBlogger.net. Started by the same person who founded the above photography school, ProBlogger.net shares extensive information and weekly instructional videos on the process of launching, growing, marketing, and profiting from blogging.

- SBA.gov. For those whose education includes bumping up their business know-how, this website, run by the Small Business Administration, provides a wealth of information about planning, funding, starting, managing, and growing a small business.

- WarriorForum.com. This massive online forum is a tremendous resource for anyone interested in learning about online marketing and copywriting. It's not only populated with a vast amount of information, but many of the top people in the field regularly visit and share their opinions. If you dare, you can even post links to your projects and ask for feedback. Just be sure you're ready, because you'll get a lot of extremely direct responses.

Free Online Courses

A huge chunk of formalized education is now moving online. Some courses and programs require payment, which we'll explore below, but there is also a decent amount of free, high-value online academic-quality course material. The benefit of online training is that it is self-paced, flexible, and often provides access to teachers, tools, and facilities that would normally never be available to most people. We've already seen some of these more formalized courses hosted at iTunes and other websites.

Recently, the Massachusetts Institute of Technology took the notion of free online education to an entirely different level with the launch of their OpenCourseWare (OCW) Consortium. Now boasting more than one hundred prominent institutions worldwide, the OCW has become a massive movement with a lot of momentum. OCW Consortium members, including the likes of MIT, Berkeley, Tufts, Carnegie Melon, Yale, Notre Dame, Johns Hopkins, and UMass–Boston are collectively making the lectures and materials from thousands of courses available to the public for free. You can find detailed information and links to each university's programs and search for courses by topic at http://www.ocwconsortium.org/index.php.

Access to this level of instruction and information for free is simply unprecedented, so if you choose to take advantage of it, I would encourage you to also make a donation at whatever level is right for you to keep the OCW movement alive.

Books, DVDs, Magazines, and Newspapers

Now we're adding a modest financial investment to the equation. Find all the magazines that cover your area of interest and immerse yourself in them. The more, the better. Over time, you'll begin to figure out which ones are most useful and which are largely redundant or not useful enough to justify the time and effort.

Then go to your online or local bookstore, find out what the top-selling or most-recommended titles are in the area of your passion and dive in. Commit to the process of learning by setting a reading schedule and take notes to ensure active involvement in the process.

While subject-specific content is increasingly easy to find online and in magazines, my experience has been that comprehensive business, entrepreneurship, and legal information is still best presented in a book format, where you can take your time and build your knowledge, chapter by chapter. Tap websites, magazines, and blogs to supplement your knowledge, but start with the more methodical approach you'll find in books.

A caveat: If you're looking for Internet business or e-commerce education, you should focus most of your reading online. The rules of the online-business game change so quickly that by the time a book hits the shelves much of the information may be dated.

Final renegade tip: Explore the career section of the bookstore. You may be able to find courses, training manuals, or DVDs that will guide you through an entire training/certification program and even prepare you to take exams, if needed.

Paid Online Courses

With widespread adoption of broadband Internet access, educational institutions around the world are clamoring for their slice of the distance-learning pie, and you are the beneficiary. In fact, it is becoming increasingly easy to attain a degree completely online.

Distance learning or online courses tend to come in four flavors:

- Self-paced. These are usually some combination of written materials and prerecorded video or audio that are made available 24/7 and can be perused on your schedule.

- Virtual lectures: These courses designate a set schedule of lectures that will be webcast online, assignments that must be handed in (by e-mail), and exams that are taken either on- or offline and submitted for grading. The webcasting technology often requires you to sign in to class and also offers the opportunity to ask questions with the teacher and interact.

- Hybrid online: This format blends the two above modalities.

- Hybrid online/offline: Similar to the hybrid model, but requires occasional scheduled live attendance, in addition to online class attendance. For example, the master's degree in applied positive psychology at the University of Pennsylvania uses this format, offering virtual lectures, while also requiring students to gather with each other and the faculty in person, at regular intervals. Many executive MBA programs are adopting this format as well.

The big differences between these types of programs and the courses offered through the OCW Consortium are access to the teachers and the ability to pursue a degree or certification, if desired. And, the obvious downsides are the expense as well as the innate limitations of distance learning. For example, it would be difficult to teach a highly mechanical skill like motor vehicle repair in a purely distance-learning format, because it requires you to get your hands on the subject.

If you choose distance learning be sure to check out the provider before you register or pay. While there are many reputable education providers online, there is also a growing cadre of providers who are serving up a less than satisfying experience. The good news is you can find a lot of feedback online, both positive and negative, by simply searching on the provider, teacher, and the keywords "feedback," "reviews," "scam," "ratings," or "complaints."

Attend Live Trainings, Courses, or Conferences

When I wanted to learn about direct-response copywriting, I went online and searched for every variation of those words. Then, I searched on related terms, like "Internet marketing," "sales-letters," "direct-mail," and "marketer." These searches exposed me to a huge amount of information. I found the websites and blogs of a dozen or so top copywriters. I read every webpage and blog post and took notes.

Then, I found hundreds of other websites and blogs that referenced these guys and their work. I also learned a top copywriter has the potential to make a giant living and the cost of entry is not a degree, but rather knowledge, ability, and really hard work. I do hard work well so that made me happy.

From there, I found samples of writing from the A-listers, began to analyze how they wrote, and contrasted similarities and differences. I hadn't yet spent a dime, but I'd learned a ton.

Many of these top copywriters offered high-priced live trainings, but I wasn't convinced I needed to part with thousands of dollars to learn everything I needed to know. So, I moved on to books. I bought every book that was mentioned by any of the A-listers or consistently referred to in copywriting forums and devoured them.

The knowledge was pouring in and, happily, I grew more engaged by the process with each new bit of information. I began to write my own copy and play with it in my own businesses. The results blew me away. Shortly after I rewrote the webpage for Sonic Yoga's teacher training institute, enrollment nearly doubled.

Still, I knew I was capable of so much more. But, I had questions, lots of them. For me, the online forums were too impersonal, so I looked again at those live trainings. Finally, I gave in and attended a training led by one of those A-listers.

I was the newbie in a roomful of pros. I didn't care, I was there to learn . . . and try not to embarrass myself too much. Three days later, I was thinking and writing on a level it would have taken me years to reach had I stuck to my go-it-alone guns.

I am not someone who likes to surrender to the notion that I need help. I've always pretty much mastered whatever I needed to master on my own. This experience, though, opened my eyes both to the importance of finding a mentor, seeking out live attention, and copping to the fact that I don't know everything. It also made me realize how much more easily so many prior achievements could have come had I been open to help from the right people.

It is, indeed, possible to acquire vast amounts of knowledge online and on paper, but certain other bodies of knowledge are best acquired in person. So, if you need to take your knowledge, skills, and abilities to a different level and you've done everything you can, your best next step may very well be live training.

It can come in many forms: A brief workshop, an extended course, a mentoring or coaching relationship, a part-time internship, or even a volunteer position. Consider anything that will serve as a catalyst to your quest to acquire knowledge, even if it means paying more than you thought you'd ever pay. If doing so takes you a giant step closer to your dream, make it happen.

THIRTEEN

Launching Your Quest for Authority

REGARDLESS OF YOUR CHOSEN career path, acquiring public-expert status leapfrogs you to the head of the pack. It positions you as an authority, and authority opens doors. Whether those doors lead you down a career path in someone else's company, to the creation of your own entrepreneurial path, or to a growing following that lines up to buy whatever you decide to sell, these days, being known is the next most important thing to actually knowing what you're doing. Your platform is your career renegade secret marketing weapon.

Pedigrees Are So Nineties

In the past, building widespread authority and a giant platform capable of producing real opportunity; attracting friends, followers, and customers; and generating a substantial income took a lot of time, money, connections, and effort. Pedigrees and formal training carried a lot of weight. And, as we've already discussed, in certain professions, these things are still very much a necessity.

But, increasingly, authority or expert status is something that can be acquired in far more creative ways.

With the explosion of blogging, along with a growing array of conversation facilitating technology, it is now possible to establish yourself as an authority with massive reach in lightning fast time. You can do it not by pointing to a degree or pedigree, but by publicly demonstrating eyebrow-raising mastery and value, mixing it with a bit of entertainment, then using technology to rapidly distribute your message.

In the next three chapters, we'll explore how to blend leading-edge communications and marketing technologies with age-old PR techniques to demonstrate and broadcast your mastery to the world.

The first stop on our expert-authority train is blogging.

Blogging

Confession time. Though I consider myself fairly tech-savvy, it wasn't so long ago that I had no idea what a blog was. Nor, even today, do many of my friends or family know, though they are aware that I spend a fair amount of time doing it, whatever *it* is.

The word "blog" is short for web log. Blogs are essentially websites that allow a person, a blogger, or a team of bloggers, to post new entries on a website as often as they like and have older entries archived and available for viewing at the click of a button. The software that runs most blogs is now so robust and user-friendly, nearly anyone can publish, manage, or post new content in a matter of minutes.

Your blog is also the cornerstone of your campaign to establish widespread authority on any topic. It is a place that allows you to write, post, and promote the type of extensive, well-researched, thought-leading content that builds your reputation as a person of expertise, influence, and ability.

Anita's Story
Turning Offline Success into
Online Pundit Status

Former Bell & Howell lawyer turned tech-CEO turned small-business blogger Anita Campbell found this out firsthand with the launch of her blog at SmallBizTrends.com. Anita lived and breathed small business.

But she didn't just love running a business, she also loved to read about it, speak about it, write about it, and essentially talk about it to anyone who'd listen. She was a hard-core small-biz maven.

When the dot-com bubble burst, the company she helped found was sold and she decided to explore a career as a small business pundit. But there was a problem. Nobody outside of her immediate circle of friends, colleagues, and industry niche had ever heard of her.

She wasn't a published author or a popular speaker. She hadn't led a revolution in any high-profile field or launched any mega-companies. She wasn't a regular guest on any television or radio shows. Nor did she write for any newspapers or magazines. But, still, she knew she had a lot to offer those looking to launch and grow their own businesses and she had a unique way of looking at the challenges and environment of small business growth.

She began consulting, first just as a way to help friends and, eventually, as a way to earn a living. Looking to take her message and reputation to a different level, in 2003, Anita launched a blog at Small BizTrends.com and began to write about small business.

Readers came to her blog to read her original take on entrepreneurship and insightful commentary. First they came in trickles and then in droves. Some came through search engines, like Google and Yahoo!, others through links from other blogs or word of mouth. As the blogging community began to gain steam, Anita's position as a small-business blogger led to appearances in print media, on radio, and at conferences and that offline exposure brought even more notoriety to the blog, which fed the upward spiral.

As I write this, some four years after launching, SmallBizTrends.com has a massive following. The authority generated by Anita's blog led to the launch of a regular radio show and newspaper and magazine columns. Anita is also regularly asked to be a spokesperson and evangelist for a wide variety of organizations of all sizes.

In addition to the many offline sources of revenue the blog has created, it also generates substantial advertising and sponsorship revenue from Fortune 500 partners.

Simply put, Anita's got juice—and lots of it. Not because of her law degree, but because she was willing to do the work necessary to become an expert in her area, create her own limelight, and build her own voice, using the power of technology.

She didn't wait around for anyone else to determine she was worthy of a platform. Instead, she stepped up and created her own outlet, built her own audience, and grew her own platform. Now her blog is not only the center of her business, it's also her most important marketing and publicity tool.

Launching Your Blog

We talked about how to build a community around your passion through a blog in chapter 3, but now I'm going to show you how to set one up. Anyone can launch a blog in the blink of an eye. You can launch a basic blog in about fifteen minutes and have your first post online in less than an hour. And, you don't need a lick of Web-development skills.

Blogs are run with special software or "platforms" that makes the process of being a blogger about as easy as creating a document in Microsoft Word. The three leading blog platforms are Blogger, Typepad, and Wordpress.

- Blogger.com. To launch a blog using the Blogger platform, just go to Blogger.com. This service is actually owned by Google. You can sign up for an account; pick a design from their standard templates; add any special features, like pictures, videos, or audio files; write your first post; hit the publish button; and you'll be an official blogger. The big benefits of using blogger are (a) it's free, (b) it is incredibly easy to use, and (c) your blog can be hosted seamlessly on their computers, so you do not need to pay any hosting fees. The downside is that the design selections are very limited, there is little flexibility with features and options and, even though it's free, your URL or blog's Web address will be a subdomain of blogspot. So, if I used blogger for my Career Renegade blog, the actual domain name would be careerrenegade .blogspot.com. And, Blogger would own that domain, not me. You can actually set up your blog so that it uses the Blogger platform, but appears on your own domain. That would require you to pay hosting fees for your own website, though, and if you are going to pay your hosting fees I have better options for you.

- Typepad.com/Moveable-type. Moveable-Type is a far more robust blogging platform with a lot more options than Blogger.com, including more designs and better ability to customize the look and feel of each design, better management features, mobile support (iPhone and iPod Touch), and social media integration. You can have the blogging software installed on the computer that hosts any domain you own or, similar to Blogger.com, you can take the easy way and have them do everything for you through their Typepad .com blog-hosting service. While Typepad.com offers more customization, they charge a monthly fee ($4.95 to $89.95 as of this writing), and they, too, give you a subdomain. So, if my blog were hosted by Typepad, the domain would be something like careerrenegade.typepad.com. They would own the domain, not me.

- Wordpress.com and Wordpress.org. The Wordpress blogging platform's popularity has exploded in the last few years. It is massively customizable. You can choose from thousands of free and low-cost designs or create your own from scratch and it has a giant developer-base writing scripts called plug-ins that do everything from filtering spam from your comments to welcoming first-time visitors. Wordpress designs are called themes and you can find many free or very affordable themes online by just searching for "wordpress themes" or browsing the theme listing at Wordpress .COM. You can, of course, always have your design created, built, and installed for you (as I have), but it's not necessary.

To use the Wordpress platform, you can go to Wordpress.ORG, download it, and install it on your website's computers. If you're not tech-savvy, I would have someone who knows a bit about this do it for you. Many website hosting companies actually now have Wordpress already installed and all you have to do is ask them to make sure it's activated on your domain or use the control panel in the administrative area to do it yourself. Similar to Blogger and Typepad, Wordpress has its own hosted version at Wordpress.COM. You can go there, sign up for an account, choose your design (theme), customize it, and be blogging for free in minutes.

Getting Started on Your Blog

First, read a bunch of top blogs to see how the best people do it. You can find them at Technorati.com, ranked in order of popularity. Look at the top one hundred and see how they do it. Then choose one of the free blogging platforms to play with. Set up an account, get a feel for how they work, choose a name, and just start writing.

Take anywhere from a few days to a few weeks. Start to suss out what you want to write about, what topics hold the greatest interest for you, and whether you feel you know enough to add substantial value to the niche you'd like to eventually become known in. Spend some time reading the blogs I've listed in the resources below to get a better understanding of the process and culture of blogging. There is a protocol and an etiquette to blogging and you'll want to know them.

For example, it's not a great idea to approach an A-list blogger with a request for a link to your blog until you've already shown them a lot of love by linking to them, writing about them in your blog, or developing a relationship with them. No doubt, you'll break some rules, we all do. But, the more you know, the better off you'll be.

I'll share a bunch of resources below to help get you up to speed as quickly as possible, but you might also try reaching out to more established bloggers to ask for advice. When I was getting ready to launch my first blog, I reached out to popular bloggers, Penelope Trunk (BrazenCareerist.com), Maki (DoshDosh.com), and Tamar Weinberg (Techipedia .com). Though they were already well-known and I was a total newbie, they took the time to share some great insights and answered my questions. The blogosphere tends to be that way; it's part of the ethic, bloggers helping bloggers.

Once you feel ready, go to GoDaddy.com, search for a domain name you like and reserve it. You can then set up your blog and start blogging in earnest.

One final bit of advice, make sure the topic you choose to blog on is not only something you want to become known for, but something you feel passionate about. Blogging is hard work and, without passion for your niche, it will get old really quickly.

Here is a short list of resources to get you going. Because the tools, rules, and technology behind launching and growing a blog evolve daily, I'd recommend spending more time reading blogs about blogging than books about blogging.

Blogs with Great Content about Blogging

ProBlogger.net

DoshDosh.com

Performancing.com

ReadWriteWeb.com

CopyBlogger.com

Successful-Blog.com

Micropersuasion.com

SethsBlog.com

SEOMoz.com

SearchEngineGuide.com

Wordpress.com/Wordpress.org

Blogger.com

Typepad.com

Entrepreneurs-Journey.com

DailyBlogTips.com

Skelliewag.org

ChrisG.com

ChrisBrogan.com

37signals.com/svn/

Lifehacker.com

Sparkplugging.com

MenWithPens.ca

Remarkablogger.com

Techipedia.com

SOBEvent.com

SmashingMagazine.com

Books

- *Blogging Tips: What Bloggers Won't Tell You About Blogging* by Lorelle VanFossen (SplashPress, 2007)

- *The New Rules of Marketing and PR* by David Meerman Scott, (Wiley, 2007)
- *Naked Conversations: How Blogs Are Changing the Way Businesses Talk with Customers* by Robert Scoble (Wiley, 2006)
- *ProBlogger: Secrets for Blogging Your Way to a Six-Figure Income* by Darren Rowse and Chris Garrett (Wiley, 2008)

Guest Posting and Contributing to Popular Blogs

Editors of high-traffic blogs and websites have a tough job. Day in, day out, they are engaged in a quest to find content that is valuable and distinct enough to keep their readers coming back. If you can provide that content, you not only make their jobs easier, you also benefit from exposure to massive numbers of people and the implicit authority that comes from appearing on a respected blog or website.

This very technique was leveraged by Guam-based newspaper and speechwriter turned pro-blogger, Leo Babauta, with stunning results. Soon after launching ZenHabits.net in 2007, Leo began guest posting all over the Web, starting small, then, as his reputation grew, writing for bigger and bigger outlets. This exposed him to hundreds of thousands of new readers and top social-media submitters, who began to champion his content, taking his profile to new heights. We'll learn more about Leo's incredible journey in a bit.

How to approach bloggers and blog editors to guest post or contribute: Compared to traditional media outlets, bloggers tend to be far more approachable. A great way to get the attention of a blogger or blog editor is to invest in the community. Show your interest in the blog's content and community by reading it and sharing relevant, meaningful, thoughtful comments on the blog. If you can't muster the will to do that, then you probably don't feel strongly enough about the content area or blog to contribute substantial value in the form of an article or post.

Doing this for a few weeks, or even months, before approaching with a request to contribute also cultivates a certain amount of name recognition with both the blogger and the readers. So, when it comes time to ask about guest posting or contributing, you are much more likely to be considered.

During this same period of time, you should be posting your best possible content at your own blog, because, eventually, when your name keeps popping up next to thoughtful comments, the blogger or editor will click over to your blog to see who you are.

Finally, if the blog you'd like to write for has a contributor or guest-posting policy, be sure to follow it. If not, use the contact form or e-mail to offer to guest post. Rather than offering your general guest-posting services, offer a very specific topic or article that you know would be highly relevant to the blog's readers. For example, when I approached the editor of FreelanceSwitch.com, which has a huge readership of freelancers in many fields, I offered to write an article on marketing and sales tips for freelancers. Approaching bloggers this way will dramatically increase your likelihood of success.

Guest-posting resource: Blogs are ranked and categorized by a number of different services, so start your search for the most relevant, widely read blogs to approach with the list below, then follow links on the bigger blogs to find other relevant blogs.

Technorati.com

AllTop.com

Blogsearch.Google.com

BlogLines.com

MyBlogLog.com

BlogZoom.com

BlogCatalog.com

Google.com/reader

Riding the Content-Aggregation Wave

Here's one last technique I've used to build authority in a variety of ways, most recently in the world of blogging.

When I launched my blog, I knew nothing about blogging. But, five weeks later, an article I wrote on marketing your blog hit the front page of one of the largest social media hubs and sent more than twenty thousand visitors to the blog over a one-week period.

Why did people care what I had to say? The funny thing is . . . they didn't!

The post that landed so much attention was a roundup post. I wanted to know what the best way to market a blog was, so I e-mailed a selection of top bloggers and asked if they'd mind contributing their thoughts to an article. I got a terrific set of responses.

I then turned this into an extensive roundup article featuring all of their super-informative thoughts and added my own ideas at the end. The article was packed with value and was so well received, I have since then turned it into a regular column, added a wider range of bloggers and tech-celebs, and continued to add my own observation and spin at the end of each. Now people have started to come to me to ask my advice in launching and marketing blogs.

The point is that even when you feel you don't yet have

enough value or a big enough story to offer, you may be able to aggregate the wisdom of others around a high-interest topic, throw in a bit of your own thoughts and ride the coattails of other peoples' authority until you've established enough of your own.

A second approach to building authority through aggregation is to become an information filter. In any given industry or niche, there is far too much information for the average person to digest on a daily basis.

I follow about one hundred and fifty to two hundred blogs. Legendary human filters like Scobleizer.com's Robert Scoble have at times tracked more than six hundred blogs and websites. But your average person who can't count reading blogs as part of her or his job only has time for a handful, maybe a few dozen tops, so when you find people who follow all the news in a particular area, filter what's most important, and then share it on their blog in edited, bullet-points with links to the original for detail, it's like manna from digi-heaven. It lets you stay up-to-date without giving up your life.

And, the good news is, becoming a filter only requires two things: time and enough fundamental industry knowledge to be able to separate the wheat from the chaff.

Some of the top blogs and bloggers have made their reputations largely as human filters, then turned those reputations into opportunity. Plus, an interesting thing happens when you become a filter: You are exposed to such a huge volume of information that over time you know enough to make the transition from filter to source.

Micro-Blogging

Blogs are great places for authoritative, resource-laden, high-value articles that aggregate content in a single, easily searchable and readable place. They are also set up well to be optimized and fed into the major search engines, making you and your content easily discoverable.

But, as the world becomes more mobile, people increasingly demand content in a format that is portable and easy to digest in the blink of an eye. Enter micro-blogging. Senior vice president and director of Insight at Edelman Digital and author of the Micropersuasion.com blog Steve Rubel compares blogging and micro-blogging to golf, calling blogging your long game and micro-blogging your short game. The better you are at each, the better your overall game becomes.

Micro-blogging is best explained by looking at how the premier micro-blogging platform, Twitter (www.twitter .com) works. When you visit Twitter.com, you can sign up for a free account, then activate the Twitter communication system on your computer, IM, or cell-phone. Once you have your account, you can search for other friends and sign up to *follow* them. They can do the same with you. Now, you're ready to start *tweeting*.

Tweeting is like sending mini-blog posts, micro-bursts of information (up to 140 characters or about fifteen to twenty words) that are immediately *pushed* to your followers in *their preferred mode of reception*. For many people who tweet, that preferred mode is cell phone. It lets people share small chunks of information with an audience of followers all day long by cell phone. The system keeps a record of all of your outgoing and incoming tweets, making them archivable and searchable not only by you, but by major search engines.

I might be sitting at a café, reading an article at lunch when I stumble upon an amazing quote or reference. I can whip out my cell phone, tweet "great recipe in *Cooking Light* mag for healthy apple pie." Or, maybe I'd just want to share that "I am eating the best apple pie in NYC at blah-blah restaurant on Broadway."

The potential applications for Twitter and other micro-blogging platforms are still in their infancy. The tech world is all over it. When I was at last year's South By Southwest Interactive conference in Austin, you had to be on Twitter if you wanted any hope of knowing where the best panels, people, and parties were in real time.

Just as blogs exploded into the mainstream world after saturating the tech world a few years ago, micro-blogging is poised to make a similar leap, because of its ultra portability and easy-to-digest short messages. While the system is used by many to share the events of daily life, a growing cadre of early adopters are beginning to tap micro-blogging as a powerful authority-building adjunct to blogging.

Bloggers and tech-oriented journalists have begun to mine Twitter as a source for information and quotes for articles and posts. Find those people, follow them, interact intelligently, offer value, and you just might find yourself quoted in their next article.

As I write this, Rubel, for example, follows about three hundred people, but has more than eight thousand people following his tweets. Part of this is because he is an interactive-media maven who digests information from more than four hundred blogs, edits, and then tweets the important stuff in short bursts to his followers. He uses his popular blog, Micropersuasion.com, for his longer, resource-laden articles and more detailed analysis and Twitter for quick connections. In fact, on any given day, Rubel might tweet dozens of times. A recent survey of his audience revealed that while 90 percent of his Twitter followers read his blog, only 50 percent of his blog readers follow his tweets. So, while there is some crossover, there is a sizable chunk of his total audience that sticks to a single medium. Maximizing both accelerates the expansion of both his overall audience and his authority.

Blogging and micro-blogging also allow you to connect with people who might otherwise never take your call.

You can find me on Twitter at www.Twitter.com/jonathan fields. Go there now, get your free account, and click the "follow" button to keep up with me throughout the day.

Micro-Blogging Resources

Twitter.com

Pownce.com

Jaiku.com

Plurk.com

The Big Juicy Twitter Guide, Caroline-middlebrook .com/blog/category/twitter-guide/

FOURTEEN

Getting Social Online

THERE ARE TWO MAJOR TYPES of social-media hubs, those that emphasize conversation, connecting, and networking and those based around content promotion. The former category includes websites like Facebook.com, MySpace.com, and LinkedIn.com, where the primary purpose is to facilitate conversation. The latter includes the much less known (at least to the nontech world), though mind-blowingly powerful content-promotion hubs, including Digg.com, Reddit.com, StumbleUpon.com, Mixx.com, and Y! Buzz. Let's start with the big three.

Making Friends Online: Facebook.com, LinkedIn.com, and MySpace.com

These three websites are the heavy-hitters in the world of conversation and networking-driven online communities. Collectively, they boast hundreds of millions of members (Facebook has more than seventy million, LinkedIn exceeds twenty million, and MySpace boasts more than two hundred million), they are free to join, and each has its own culture.

Facebook.com

With more than seventy million members, Facebook is growing at lightning speed. And, though it originally caught fire among the college set, the fastest growing demographic is now the over-twenty-five age bracket. Facebook offers a very clean interface and a vast library of applications (apps) that may be installed with the click of a mouse to customize and facilitate almost any conversation or transaction.

Favorite apps include BlogFuse, which lets you publish your blog posts to your Facebook page; Twitter, which lets you post your latest tweets (see above); My Questions, which lets you broadcast questions to your friends and gather information; and HobNob!, an app that lets you post the name of a person you'd like to connect with and then broadcasts that request to expanding waves of friends, increasing the likelihood that your message will eventually get to someone who can make an introduction. You can search for these and other apps in the application directory in the left margin of your profile page.

Facebook also boasts more than ten thousand groups. Groups are like clubs, each with its own topic area, culture, and rules. You can search for and join the groups most relevant to the area you are interested in building credibility within. Make sure to participate actively by joining in discussions between group members, offering insights and information, and attending live meet-ups so you can become known within the group.

You can also find people with similar interests, send messages, and "friend" them. Then, stay in touch. Remember, you won't gain any recognition if you sign up, install a bunch of apps, friend a bunch of people, join a bunch of groups, then check your Facebook page once a month. One of the fundamental rules across all social-media platforms is to contribute and participate. Do that and everything falls into place.

My Facebook name is Jonathan Fields. Be sure to visit my profile, then friend me and join my career renegade

Facebook group. For more information on Facebook.com, check out Jason Alba and Jesse Stay's *I'm on Facebook, Now What???* (Happy About, 2008).

LinkedIn.com

LinkedIn started as a small, professional networking community, largely targeted at the IT world. It quickly gained acclaim as the serious place to be for grown-ups looking for high-level connections and career opportunities. It stayed fairly small for a number of years, before taking off over the last three years. The focus remains decidedly more business oriented and the average user is likely to be in their thirties or older.

LinkedIn allows you to create a detailed profile page, with a focus on career and professional skills and abilities.

LinkedIn boasts two killer authority-building features. One is LinkedIn Answers, which you can find at LinkedIn.com/answers. This section of the website allows members to post questions and assign them to certain categories. For those looking to build authority, a daily visit to this section will reveal the types of questions being asked. Look for questions whose answers will allow you to demonstrate your expertise, then post the most useful answer possible. Your answer will be seen not only by the person who posted the question, but by anyone else who clicks on it for seven days. Every time you provide expert answers, you also earn expertise that can get you featured on the LinkedIn Answers home page.

A second great way to leverage your LinkedIn profile to grow your authority is to request people who you have helped to review and recommend you. You can also join groups, but don't bother joining unless you are willing to commit to being active.

My LinkedIn ID is Jonathan Fields. Be sure to join my network by sending an invite. For more info on tapping the authority-building power of LinkedIn, Jason Alba also wrote a great short guide, called *I'm on LinkedIn: Now What???* (Happy About, 2007).

MySpace.com

MySpace's roots are in music and multimedia. It's a great place to connect with like-minded people, especially if you're under twenty-five. It's also a great place to discover indie music and video, but unless you are looking to establish your authority in those worlds using the techniques established above, you'll be better served allocating your energy to Facebook and LinkedIn.

Sharing, Talking About, and Promoting Killer Content

I was only a few weeks into my own career as a blogger when my first article hit the front page of Digg.com. I didn't really get what Digg.com was back then, save the fact that it drove so much traffic to my site that it immediately crashed the blog and it took the better part of a day to get it back online.

Digg.com is one example, maybe the largest, of a vote-driven social-media hub. It is a place where anyone can grab a free account, then submit any content they find anywhere online for consideration by the other members of the community. If the members like it, they can vote it up, if not they can either do nothing or bury it. And, anyone can comment on it.

If an article gets enough up votes in a short period of time, it is promoted to the front page where it can reside for anywhere from a few hours to a day or so. Once on the front page, millions of people see it and thousands click through to read it. Then other websites and bloggers link to it, driving a second wave of traffic.

Digg.com is only one example of a vote-driven social-media hub. Many other communities, with tens of millions of participants have emerged, each with its own culture, ethics, emphasis, and rules.

Though immensely effective at driving traffic to web-sites, most social-media hubs that revolve around content promotion are still heavily weighted and influenced by those in the tech world. You need a certain amount of savvy just to know they exist, let alone understand how to tap their power.

In February 2008, though, that may have changed in a massive way with the launch of the Y! Buzz content-promotion hub at Buzz.Yahoo.com. Anyone with a Yahoo! account can submit content for voting. If an article gets pop-ular enough, it can then be promoted to the Yahoo! home page, which exposes the article not just to the tech-savvy social-media crowd, but one of the biggest mainstream au-diences on the Web.

The impact of hitting the Yahoo! home page dwarfs the traffic that can be delivered by any other content-promotion hub out there. The already hugely popular Salon.com re-ported one million unique visitors on the day one of its ar-ticles was promoted to the Yahoo! home page via Y! Buzz, representing the single biggest traffic day in its twelve-year history. Similarly, TechCrunch.com reported their highest-ever traffic day, along with one thousand comments the day a single post was promoted by Y! Buzz. Y! Buzz is still in *beta* (early stage with limited features and content, designed to get feedback), but should be fully operational by the time you read this, with substantially more content and explanation available on participation. Be sure to check Career Renegade.com for the latest information on Y! Buzz.

So, what is the best way to tap these social-media hubs to build your authority?

Steve Rubel recommends creating a presence in multiple communities, using the "don't place all your eggs in one basket" philosophy. His reasoning is simple. Tech solutions and, often, entire communities, tend to have short lives. You never know what will survive, so spreading yourself across multiple platforms and communities gives you a better chance of weathering a certain amount of expected communal extinction.

Social-media power-user, uber-maven and blogger Muhammad Saleem adds:

There are two key things you have to do and everything else is simply ancillary. The first is to participate and be a member in good standing in whatever it is you want to be an authority on. And the second is to join the conversation. For example one of the things I want to learn more about is how search works (and more specifically social search). So I would start by reading up on it, then actually implementing it and analyzing the results, and then sharing the results with other people, getting their feedback, and even giving my opinion on what they have to say on the matter.

Steve and Muhammad have the ability to devote a lot of time to these communities, because doing so is at the heart of how they earn their livings. But, what if you have an unrelated full-time job and other obligations that leave little time to develop profiles in multiple communities and become an active participant in each?

My approach has been to focus on a smaller number of communities, for me it's StumbleUpon.com and Twitter .com, and build my profiles by regularly finding and sharing great content with both my StumbleUpon friends and the great StumbleUpon community. Same thing for Twitter.

In fact, what started as a way to build authority has quickly grown into a place where I've found not only wonderful content, but a growing family of friends from all over the world.

With so many communities and groups of friends or followers in each community, a new generation of "lifestreaming" services now offers to aggregate all the communications with all friends across many different communities into one place. The front-runner as of this writing is FriendFeed .com with SocialThing.com on it's heels. Each serves your community-aggregating needs somewhat differently and by the time this book hits the shelves, the feature sets will likely have evolved substantially and new lifestreaming services may have gained favor. So, my best advice is to check out both, Google "lifestreaming" to find the latest entrants and reviews and see what might work best for you.

Social-Media Conversation-Driven Hubs

Facebook.com—friend me, I am Jonathan Fields on Facebook

MySpace.com

LinkedIn.com—connect with me, I am Jonathan Fields on LinkedIn

Flickr.com

YouTube.com—connect with me, I am CareerRenegade on YouTube.com

Revver.com

Video.google.com

Metacafe.com

Vimeo.com

Major Social-Media Content-Promotion Hubs

Digg.com—friend me, I am JonathanFields on Digg

StumbleUpon.com—friend me, I am Jonathan-Fields on StumbleUpon

Reddit.com

Sphinn.com—friend me, I am JonathanFields on Sphinn

Mixx.com—friend me, I am JonathanFields at Mixx

Buzz.yahoo.com (Y! Buzz)

Propeller.com

Bebo.com

Lifestreaming/Community Aggregators

FriendFeed.com—friend me, I am jonathanfields at friendfeed

Utterz.com

SocialThing.com

Social Bookmarking

There's one last online social content–sharing tool you should consider exploring, social bookmarking. You know how when you find a great article online, you can bookmark or favorite the page on your Web browser? Well, there are now online services that provide that same bookmarking functionality, but instead of storing the links on your computer, they store them online, so you can access them anytime from any computer.

The eight-hundred-pound gorilla in this space is a service called De.licio.us (which is also the domain name).

De.licio.us allows you to sign up for a free account, then begin saving all your favorite links to your account. It's a fantastic service to save and categorize information. But De.licio.us can also be used as a potential tool to encourage content you create to become viral and be bookmarked and shared by thousands of people in the blink of an eye. Here's how.

People tend to bookmark certain types of content: photos, videos, insightful or entertaining articles. But articles packed with valuable resources, tips and links also tend to get bookmarked. The longer the article, the more likely it is to be bookmarked, because it becomes a resource that people might not be able to finish reading in one sitting and will want to come back to again and again to use as a reference. The proviso is, of course, that the resources, tips, and links must have genuine value and relevance.

While De.licio.us is an online bookmarking service, it also has its own content-promotion system. It keeps track of how many people are bookmarking any given piece of content at any given time. Content that is bookmarked very quickly by a lot of people begins to rise up the De.licio.us hotlist. If it gets enough bookmarks fast enough, it hits the hotlist front page and that can generate thousands of new visits, which often turns into even more bookmarks and links.

A great way to tap the power of social bookmarking is

to create extensive advice-driven articles on your blog that both demonstrate your expertise and offer up a mountain of resources and direct links to those resources, get the word out through your readers, relationships, and your chosen social-media communities and encourage people to bookmark the content through De.licio.us.

Be sure to check the updated resource lists at Career Renegade.com for the latest developments.

FIFTEEN

Building on Blogging and Social Media

BLOGGING, MICRO-BLOGGING, AND social media will form the core of your online authority- and relationship-building campaign, but there are a handful of additional tools and techniques that can really turbocharge your quest to become known as the go-to person in the area of your passion.

Podcasting, Internet Radio, and Blog Talk Radio

How cool would it be to be able to broadcast your own radio or TV show to a growing list of show subscribers as often as you'd like and have show archives available for hundreds of millions of people to download at will? Do you think that might help spread your message and build your reputation and following? Enter podcasting and blog talk radio.

Podcasting is a fancy name for recording an audio or video show (using similar techniques mentioned in chapter 3), and getting it listed on iTunes, where millions of people can find your show, sample an episode, then subscribe to have future episodes automatically downloaded to their computers and iPods.

Back in 2005, Texan Luria Petrucci and her husband created a daily video podcast, GeekBrief.TV. Each show features Luria as her cyber alter ego, Cali Lewis, talking about breaking tech news. The show was an instant smash, generating such a huge following that, within weeks, their computers couldn't handle the traffic. And, more recently, GeekBrief.TV has attracted the attention of large corporate sponsors. Beyond the financial opportunity, though, Cali has built a huge public following, though she very much prefers the phrase "friends of the show." Whatever you call it, Cali's got the ears, eyes, and even hearts of a sizable number of people.

While podcasting now boasts video capability, you can also create audio-only podcasts and produce and edit them in the format of a traditional radio show. A search in iTunes will reveal thousands of podcasts adopting the radio show format. One limitation to this format, however, is the lack of real-time interaction with listeners. Enter BlogTalkRadio .com (BLT).

BLT is a free service that operates as a call-in Internet radio station. You can sign up to host your own online radio show, provide the details, and set a show schedule. Your show will then be listed on BLT's website and you can promote it on your various online homes. At show time, you log in to your online show control board and begin to host. The big difference between this and podcasting is that your show is also assigned telephone lines that allow listeners and guests to call in during the show. You control the call-in cue on your virtual control panel. The show is automatically recorded and made available as a podcast, too, so listeners can either join live and listen to an archived audio version. You can also promote a link to the show archive on your own site.

Here are some great resources to get you going podcasting, video podcasting, and creating an Internet call-in radio show:

BlogTalkRadio.com: Set up your own free call-in show and promote it online.

GeekBrief.TV: Cali's daily tech-news show, you can subscribe directly through iTunes at the website, too. The show is a great example of content that does well in video podcasting.

How-to-Podcast-Tutorial.com: A detailed online tutorial to get you started podcasting, covering everything from equipment needed to planning, recording, editing, publishing, and promoting your podcast.

iTunes and iPod (Apple.com): This should be self-evident, but, while other portable audio and video players are available, iPods and their content-management software dominate the market, so focus on these, not on the fringe players.

Podcasts about podcasting you can find on iTunes

podCast411

Podcast Academy

Podcasting for Dummies with Tee Morris

Adam Currie's Daily Source Code

Learn to Podcast (from Apple)

Podcasting Underground with Jason Van Orden

Podcasting for Dummies by Tee Morris. Special note: Because podcasting technology is evolving so quickly, you are probably best served by using books as background, but focusing your energy online for the most up-to-date tips, tools, and techniques.

Old School Meets New School

Using Releases for Search Engine and Google Alert Branding

Over the last ten years, I've had a lot of success getting my businesses and adventures featured in a broad variety of newspapers and magazines, from the *New York Times* to *Vogue* and the *Wall Street Journal* to *Yoga Journal*. And, while some of these placements were great for business, many also served the broader purpose of building awareness and defining a brand.

For decades, the standard approach was to pitch the influencers, who were often editors and producers, with your story and hope they'd be interested in covering it. If they were, you would then have exposure to that media outlet's readers, listeners, or viewers. The gatekeepers controlled the flow, and with mainstream media this is still very much the case.

But over the last three to five years, as you've already seen, with the explosion of the Internet, small publishers and bloggers, search technology and social media, the rules of the game have changed dramatically. The playing field, at least online, has been largely leveled.

Indeed, the flow of information is now very often reversed. Frequently, a media-worthy event gets coverage first in peer-to-peer communication technology then gets posted to the Web and then makes its way to print, radio, and television.

In traditional media, the point of entry was very often a press release or a media kit (press release, bio, and other background materials) that would be picked up by editors and producers, who would then build the content of the release into a story to be published or shown.

Press releases and media kits are still important for access to traditional media, but they now play a very different role in the quest to take your message directly to readers, listeners, and viewers online, bypassing mainstream media. Here is how it works.

How Online Press Releases, Search Engines, and Google Alerts Let You Bypass Media Outlets and Publishers and Take Your Message Straight to Millions of People

Instead of having your release mailed, faxed, FedExed, e-mailed, or otherwise transmitted to media outlets, you can now use online services to distribute your materials to tens of thousands of media outlets and publishers who have opted to receive these materials. Any one of them may then run with the story. But that's just the beginning of the impact.

Once distributed, a well-written release with a good headline is likely to be picked up by major search-engine news services, like Google.com and Yahoo.com. Once that happens, everyone who reads these services (hundreds of millions of people) will be directly exposed to your message. Sounds good, right? The story is still not over.

Once Google.com indexes your release, it will scan your headline and first sentence or two to see if any words match keywords selected by the millions of people who subscribe to Google Alerts. Google Alerts are e-mailed to tens of millions of people whenever any new story appears in any content Google indexes that has a keyword they've chosen in the headline or first few sentences. So if, for example, someone has a Google Alert for any new content that features the keywords, "career planning," anytime Google indexes content with these words prominently featured, I am going to get an e-mail.

This ability to have your releases and other content regularly pushed to millions of people who have expressed an interest in what you want to become known for goes a long way toward leveling the media playing field. It lets you bypass the editorial filters set up by mainstream media and take your message directly to your desired audience's computers in an instant. Do this on a monthly basis, provide highly relevant, extraordinarily high-value, well-written content and you will be well on your way to building your personal brand. And it costs next to nothing to do.

But, before you go banging out online releases, I have two big, fat words of caution.

First, one of the prime functions of those editors and producers, the gatekeepers of traditional media, is to craft content into a form that will be valuable and easily digested by readers and viewers. In a word, they edit what gets to their audience, so as to avoid barraging them with an endless stream of useless or poorly expressed content. People value this editing function greatly, which is the main reason mainstream media is still around.

Now millions of people have the ability to take their message straight to the audience and the great majority of the content that is delivered is a waste of time. In the "direct-to-reader" world, people do there own editing. So if you provide content that is manipulative, low-value, poorly written, unprofessional, or disrespectful in any way they will not only filter you out by ignoring you, marking your content as spam, blacklisting you, setting up e-mail rules and scripts that block you, but, if you continue to provide more of the same, the Google Alert readers may very well tap their own online communications channels to tear you a new one.

Similarly, do not send a news release directly to someone

who does most of their writing online, maintains a blog, or other online channels of communication without first establishing some kind of relationship or communication. At a very minimum, make sure you've read their blog and that your release is on point. Ask them if they'd like to receive your materials before sending them. Seek permission. Failure to do this could be viewed as spam and the last thing you want to do is make your first contact disrespectful.

Online Release and Alert Resources

PRWeb.com—online release distribution service

eReleases.com

BusinessWire.com

PRNewswire.com

Vocus.com

Google.com/alerts

Join Media-Lead Services and Groups

There's a little known secret in the publicity world, it's something the paid publicity pros would prefer you didn't know. But, it's also been behind a number of my largest media coups.

Since I've been in business, people have asked who does

my PR. When I tell them I do, they stand in disbelief. "You must have some pretty sick contacts," they say. And these days, I do. But that's not the secret and it's not what scored my early features.

Top bloggers and blog editors are constantly on the hunt for fresh content and editors and producers suffer this same, sometimes crushing, burden. What most people don't realize is that the media is desperate for great stories and insightful, entertaining, and valuable experts.

There are two ways to get the attention of blog editors and producers. The first is to seek them out. Find the editor or producer who handles the type of story you'd like to be featured in, pitch the story, and hope they bite. You might be surprised how far you can get. In fact, this is how I did it for the first few years. But, then I learned a few secrets that have allowed me to continue to be featured by mainstream media with far less effort.

ProfNET/PRLeads.com: Even after writers, editors, and producers decide to develop a story, they often need sources to provide expert information. They generally turn first to their own contacts. But many also turn to a service that every PR firm and a much smaller number of really media-savvy experts subscribe to. The service is called PR Leads and it allows you access to something called the ProfNET database on two levels.

ProfNET is a service that allows people who are developing stories for the media—writers, reporters, bloggers, editors, and producers—to post queries that summarize the story they are working on and then ask for experts in a particular topic to contact them. Those queries are then mailed out to a topic-relevant group of people who have subscribed to ProfNET not as media, but as topical experts.

The service is free for those in the media. But, to be listed as an expert, you need to subscribe. PR firms subscribe, then spend time culling all these queries (there can be hundreds every day) to see which of the experts they represent might work for a story. They'll then e-mail the person who wrote the query and pitch their expert. But you can get the same access to the ProfNET database as the PR firms and have the same opportunity to pitch *yourself* as an expert through PRLeads.com. Just sign up, choose the areas of expertise you would like to receive queries on, and wait for the e-mails to start rolling in.

Once you see a query that matches your knowledge, skills, or abilities, here is what you do:

1. Respond as quickly as possible. The moment the query is sent, any number of other experts will begin to vie for a spot in the article and, often, the first person to respond with solid information that satisfies the journalist's needs gets the feature.

2. Follow the contact instructions provided in the query, don't be cute and try to get to the source in some other way.

3. In the subject line, write, "Query response:" then add the headline from the query.

4. In the body, briefly introduce yourself, write two sentences that highlight your qualifications.

5. Provide a brief, bullet-point response, offering 75 percent of the information requested right there in your e-mail.

6. Finish by mentioning you are available for follow-up and provide direct contact information.

HelpAReporterOut.com (HARO): A friend who writes for a major New York newspaper introduced me to another resource a few months back. It started as a Facebook.com group by a guy named Peter Shankman. Peter was friends with a ton of reporters who kept calling him for sources. In an effort to make the process easier for himself, he created a group on Facebook, invited all the experts he knew to join, and then allowed his expert friends to invite new experts to the group. Then, every time one of his reporter friends needed a source, he just posted the queries to the Facebook group.

In March 2008, Peter moved the group over to the HARO website and within a week, the database of experts had grown to more than eleven thousand people. As of August 2008, more than twenty thousand experts have joined. Pretty much anyone who considers themselves an expert can join HARO and get daily press queries passed along to them.

As I write this, Peter has kept the group free, but with such rapid growth, if the work becomes too much, I can't guarantee it will stay that way. This group is for genuine, on-point sources, not random pitches or slightly relevant shots in the dark by PR pros representing a broad basket of clients.

So, before you can join, you will have to, in Peter's words, "promise not to e-mail a reporter with an answer that doesn't match what they're looking for. In other words, you won't waste a reporter's time." If a reporter rats out your off-topic pitch to Peter, you'll be quickly banned from the group.

Radio-TV Interview Report (RTIR), RTIRonline.com: ProfNET/PR Leads and HelpAReporterOut.com are great ways to expose yourself to the media. But, if you are specifically interested in appearing on radio or television, many producers turn to a publication called the *Radio-TV Interview Report* to find guests. The report comes out twice a month and also appears online. According to the publisher, about four thousand shows get the report and each issue features one hundred to one hundred and fifty authors and experts who are available for interviews. You can get listed by advertising in *RTIR* relatively inexpensively and they'll even design your ad for you.

Media Query Resources

HelpAReporterOut.com

PRLeads.com

ProfNET.com

RTIRonline.com

Do Something Others Want to Do Then Share How You Did It

Sometimes the fastest way to prove your own abilities is to go out and do something that demonstrates your mastery, then let the world know.

Legendary personal-growth guru Tony Robbins tells the story of how, as a relative unknown, he appeared on a radio show claiming to be able to instantly cure phobias through neurolinguistic programming. A woman called in to the show with a lifelong fear of snakes and he said he could cure her instantly. Then the woman's therapist called in labeling Robbins a charlatan. They agreed to meet the next day in a public place to put the phobia cure to the test and, sure enough, a short time later, the snake-fearing patient was playing with snakes. That moment not only took a massive set of cojones, it vaulted Robbins into the public eye.

Harlan's Story
Rookie Copywriter Slaughters the Pros

Confronted with an unplanned departure from his position as the principal of a private school, Rabbi Harlan Kilstein took a leap of faith. He decided to change careers and pursue his lifelong passion for the art and science of persuasion by opening a hypnosis franchise in southern Florida.

His new business venture grew nicely, but not one to wait around, it wasn't long before Harlan began to play with the stock advertisements that were provided for his use. He quickly discovered that the ads he was writing on his own drew a significantly higher response than the ones he was supposed to be using.

Harlan decided to shift gears, phasing out his hypnosis business and moving into the world of copywriting and marketing. Harlan sought out and trained with some of the top copywriters in the field and, soon after, talked his way into a massive break.

Jay Abraham, a legend in direct marketing, was in a bind. He needed copy written for a seminar. Instantly. Harlan, then an unproven rookie copywriter, but a rock-star networker, got word of the dilemma and offered to deliver powerhouse copy by the next day. It was a gamble. But he didn't have much to lose. Abraham gave him the shot and the copy he wrote was a massive home run. It launched Harlan's career and established him as a copywriter and marketer with serious chops.

Within months, Harlan found his copywriting dance card packed with high-paying clients. His income shot up, far exceeding what he could ever have made in education and, for that matter, obliterating what he thought he would ever make.

As we've seen happen with a number of others, as his reputation grew, he leveraged his newfound credibility in the copywriting and marketing world to exploit an education gap in the world of copywriting, mentoring young copywriters and entrepreneurs, and conducting high-priced seminars.

But the defining moment that launched his career was his willingness to publicly demonstrate his abilities, risk failure, and open himself up to the potential for extraordinary success.

Be Ready to Handle the Fire

The same technology that can be used to build your reputation can also be used by others to refute or even ruin it.

When you post an article on a blog or, for that matter, any online medium, people can and will reply. Sometimes in the comment section, sometimes on another blog, website, or social-media hub. You will have your supporters, but you will also have your dissenters. On the Web, everyone has a voice and everything creates a lasting, if not permanent record.

The stronger your voice, the stronger both your support and opposition will be. The shield of anonymity provided by the online environment often encourages people to be direct, aggressive, or downright brash on a level those same people would never imagine acting in person.

If you enjoy stirring things up in a public way and you believe in what you say, you may actually be able to use the ability to create widespread controversy to your advantage. While it's never been my style, many folks have done just that as a primary tool for building a notoriety. It's just part of the process. The best way to protect yourself is to make sure your quest for authority is based not on smoke and mirrors, but on expertise.

SIXTEEN

Marketing that Won't Break the Bank

WHEN IT COMES TO MARKETING, career renegades do things differently. They find ways to be remarkable and in doing so become a source of conversation and authority that drives people to become friends, clients, customers, and evangelists.

Whether you are selling yourself to the employer or partner of your dreams or looking to launch your own business, this approach is immensely powerful. As marketing mogul Seth Godin said, "Selling to people who actually want to hear from you is more effective than interrupting strangers who don't."

Beyond the conversation- and relationship-building techniques explored in the last chapter, the prime function of marketing is simply to let people know we're here, show them how we can solve a problem, and give them a way to buy.

Fundamental Approach to Career Renegade Marketing

Focus on Buzz and Facilitate Word of Mouth

Building or rebuilding your career using the principles in this book will make you worth talking about. But, if you can, try to harness your passion and innovation to create occasional bursts of extreme remarkability, then leverage your authority and relationships to get the word out and create vehicles to facilitate the spreading of your message.

People often ask me how I've gotten so much press for my various adventures without using publicists or PR firms. The answer is simple.

As we discussed in chapter 15, reporters, editors, bloggers, and journalists are constantly hungry for great stories to share. However, much of what they're pitched is either not big enough, not relevant enough, or simply not real news. When they stumble upon or ferret out real news, it's a blessing. It makes their jobs so much easier. So, when you serve it up packaged, well-crafted, and ready to go . . . it's like a gift!

From my experience getting into local media, I knew I needed a hook for my new yoga brand. But, this time, I wanted a hook with national appeal. I needed to harness all the swirling passion that defined my new business into an intense burst of remarkability that would get people talking . . . then banging down the doors. Instead of waiting for something to come along, I decided to create it.

I knew, from my days in the fitness business and, heck, just from being alive in the United States, that, at any given time, tens of millions of people wanted to lose weight. I also knew if I could tie yoga to fitness and weight loss, it would be news on a national level, which would not only be great for business, it would introduce something beneficial to so many people who might never have tried it.

So I spent a bunch of time researching, looking for studies. I found books, articles, and even videos that claimed yoga helped you lose weight. But what was glaringly absent was actual research that proved the issue.

I'd found my opening. I needed to run the first-ever study on yoga and weight loss. I approached the head of the human performance lab at Adelphi University. He wasn't convinced, but told me to come in to run a pilot study to see if it was even worth running a full study.

Completing the pilot study, I turned to face the dropped

jaws of all who were in attendance. Wow! The only question was how quickly I could get together participants for a full study. I'd set the wheels in motion.

I didn't have the money to hire any PR firms or publicists, the people with connections to editors and producers. Nor did I have any connections myself. I needed to figure out how to get the attention of top media.

I wanted exposure in mainstream health and fitness, not yoga, magazines since their reach was far wider, so I read the mastheads of the top-five fitness magazines, got the names of the right editors, and hand-delivered letters to them that revealed that we were secretly conducing the first-ever university study to measure how many calories yoga burned. Then I mentioned we wanted to offer an exclusive to the right editor.

Within hours, the fitness director of *Self* magazine called me. She wanted in. But, there was a problem. The fitness director of the country's top women's fitness magazine wanted to actually participate in the study. She wanted to be a subject.

And she wanted to be able to write about her experience. I knew that the university had strict rules about this, so, over a period of weeks, we negotiated her participation and she agreed only to release basic information and only after the university gave her the okay.

After much organizing, the university conducted the study and the results were pretty eye-opening. That alone would've made for a great story and nice image building for the studio.

But, as you now know, the story doesn't end there.

A few months before writing about the study, with me looking for ways to tap the bigger market, the fitness director called me to let me know she'd be including a small blurb in the fitness page. But she was concerned about something.

The magazine had a giant national readership and very few of its readers would be able to actually get to the New York studio to try our style of yoga. She lamented about the fact that we didn't have a video that she could recommend. Which is where it was time to take a giant leap of faith.

She wanted a video, I gave her one . . . even though none existed!

I told her that her call was quite fortuitous, because we were actually in postproduction on a new video that would offer an adapted, more moderate variation of the sequence done on the study. She asked the name and I told her it was called *Vinyasa Heat Live!* She asked the price and I said it was $19.95. She asked where people could buy it and I told her it would be available at our website.

I hung up the phone, turned to my partner and said,

"I don't know how to tell you this, but we need to film, edit, produce, and package a video in eight weeks." It took a lot of scrambling and deal making, but two months later our first run of videos arrived just as the magazine hit the shelves. The publicity from the article in *Self* sold out that run in a matter of weeks and led to the creation of four more videos and DVDs over the next few years.

Create moments of intense remarkability, then tap your network to focus their attention long enough for the virus to begin to spread.

Pay for Action, Not Advertising

I don't believe any small business should be paying to brand themselves through advertising. And, honestly, I even have trouble understanding why big companies do it, when they could spend half of their $300 million annual ad budget on innovation and differentiation on a product and service level, rather than the perception of innovation and differentiation that needs to be resold to consumers every year. But, let's not go there.

You are now armed with a veritable small business branding arsenal based in building conversation, community, and expertise. You may never need to explore more formalized advertising. If, however, you eventually do want to explore spending money to grow a bit faster, make sure every dollar spent gives you at least two dollars in sales. How? Focus your efforts on Internet marketing and direct advertising.

- Go back to our earlier discussion about PPC advertising and ClickBank from chapter 4, but instead of viewing them from the perspective of market research, now explore them from the perspective of an advertiser seeking to sell something.
- Place advertisements or links for your services or products on your websites or blogs or conversational hubs.
- Join affiliate networks. These are large networks of thousands of people who are looking to sell other peoples' stuff in exchange for a commission or percentage of the sale. ClickBank is one that focuses on infoproducts. ShareASale.com and Commission Junction.com are two large ones that allow you to post offers to pay other websites and e-mail list holders to advertise nearly any products, services, or leadforms in exchange for a commission on sales or, in the case of leads, a set fee. As an alternative, you can offer your own affiliate program and manage it yourself, with the help of any number of publicly available

affiliate-management programs (1shoppingcart.com is a popular combined affiliate-management shopping cart program and DirectTrack.com provides a highly customizable platform, too).

- Joint venture with other major list owners to launch a product, service, or business. This strategy involves partnering with people who own large lists who would be receptive to your offer and working with them to promote your business, product, or service in exchange for a healthy share of the revenue, usually in the area of 50 percent.

Learn How to Write Persuasive Copy

Career renegade paths and authority-building tools already incorporate a strong marketing element into them. The techniques and strategies in this chapter might accelerate your success, but there is likely no single greater pursuit that has had a stronger impact on my marketing and sales success than studying the art of written persuasion and copywriting.

Once you understand the fundamental principles of written persuasion, you can begin to incorporate them into everything you write and turn every word into a tool to persuade readers to move from thought to action.

Here is a list of must-read books and online resources for

anyone interested in learning the art of persuasive writing or copywriting:

Influence by Robert B. Cialdini, Ph.D. (Collins, 2006)

Tested Advertising Methods by John Caples (Prentice Hall, 1998)

Scientific Advertising by Claude C. Hopkins (FQ Classics, 2007)

Direct Mail Copy that Sells by Herschell Gordon Lewis (Prentice Hall, 1984)

Breakthrough Advertising by Eugene Schwartz (Boardroom Classics, 1984)

The Copywriter's Handbook by Robert W. Bly (Holt, 2006)

Steal This Book! by Harlan D. Kilstein, Ed.D. (Morgan James, 2005)

The Adweek Copywriting Handbook by Joseph Sugarman (Wiley, 2006)

The Ultimate Sales Letter by Dan S. Kennedy (Adams Media, 2006)

The Ultimate Marketing Plan by Dan S. Kennedy (Adams Media, 2006)

The Irresistible Offer by Mark Joyner (Wiley, 2005)

John-Carlton.com

MichelFortin.com

MakepeaceTotalPackage.com

CopyBlogger.com

Copywritersboard.com

PART 4

Let the Revolution Begin

SEVENTEEN

Cultivate the Renegade Mind-Set

I'M NOT GOING TO LIE. Failure, even when there's some great lesson to be learned and it moves us one step closer to success, just plain sucks. I know this from personal experience. Strike that, from *many* personal experiences.

The question is, though, whether it sucks badly enough to stop you from doing what you love and making a great living for the rest of your whole damn life.

My Big, Fat Failure

When I launched the yoga studio I own, my original intention was to create a business model that was reproducible and then roll out locations nationwide. So I spent a huge amount of time and money testing systems, ideas, marketing, and operating strategies. When I felt I was close enough, I took a sizable chunk of family savings, took on business debt, launched a franchise division, hired lawyers and consultants, and then worked to raise investment capital.

It took an intense year of long hours and cross-country flights to get it all legal and up and running. But, as we began to explore the model further and test it out with a "friends and family" location, it became clear there were some serious limitations in both the model and the yoga-studio market in general. I spent another two years doing everything I could, from meeting with potential investors to tweaking and adapting every possible aspect of the model. But, still, for the effort I was putting in, the universe was telling me with increasing vigor that yoga wasn't meant to work that way. It began to become clear this initiative would not become the success I had hoped for. Plus, my heart just wasn't in it anymore.

After three years of a lot of money and time lost, and a big part of my initial vision in tatters, I folded the franchise company. Was it a tough decision? Sure. An outward failure? Decidedly so. A major loss of time, money, and reputation? Well, that depends.

The business initiative failed and I certainly lost money that took a few years to make back. My wife was incredibly supportive, though we both kept dancing around this underlying notion that I was capable of so much more and failing to live up to my potential. There were many occasions where we both wanted to throw in the towel.

During those three years, though money was flowing out way faster than it was flowing in, I also learned a ton about franchise development, licensing and business opportunity law, operations and marketing, and created relationships that will serve my future efforts on a much bigger level for decades to come. It took me a year to get my main New York City studio back on track financially after spending so much time on the dream shot. This revealed the importance of not abandoning your bread-and-butter business along the way. It took me back to the importance of people and systems.

Eventually, over the next two years, I paid back the various debts incurred and now the studio serves not only as a home to a wonderful community, but as a substantial source of revenue while taking up a small enough slice of my time and energy to allow me the luxury of working on any number of other adventures.

Failure wasn't as bad as I'd imagined it to be. Very little, in terms of business risk and station in life, is completely beyond recovery. Understanding this allows you to undertake a far more rational exploration of your options. And it removes a giant excuse.

The one proviso is that, while almost anything in terms of business, money, power, toys, and reputation can be reclaimed over time, reclaiming wounded relationships is a far more complex process. Which is why I've devoted so much energy to laying out a process of getting your close friends and family not only on board any quest that will include significant risk, but fully engaged in the entire process in chapter 18.

How to Overcome Fear of Failure and Refocus on Success

A fundamental rule of life is that whatever you focus on grows. Why? Because repetition cultivates belief. This is the basis of all thought conditioning, also known as brainwashing. It's the fundamental tool of every cult. It's also the more mundane, behavioral basis behind much of the last one hundred years of metaphysical claims of transformation.

When we create a disaster scenario in our heads, then hit spin, with every repetition that scenario becomes the irrefutable outcome of our efforts. We become conditioned to believe any attempt we make at change will be destined to irreparable doom. This conditioning stops us from taking even the most fundamental steps to explore or launch a career revolution.

So, what's the answer? Rather than spending all your time obsessing about your potential failure and spinning it into some far-flung, horrific disaster scenario, take a different approach:

1. Explore and quantify failure—ONCE.
2. Explore and quantify inaction—ONCE.
3. Simulate success—DAILY.

Explore and Quantify Failure—ONCE

When we envision our potential failure, we almost never play it out realistically, but rather lean toward the irreparable doomsday scenario, the one where we not only lose every last dollar and asset, but go deeply into debt, blow apart every relationship we've had since third grade, and somehow magically purge ourselves of the knowledge, skills, and abilities that drove decades of prior success. Magnifying the impact of failure makes us feel better about not trying. It also profoundly and needlessly stunts your options, and it's a big life-limiting lie!

When you take a realistic look at your failure scenario, two things will happen. One, you'll realize it's not really as horrific or irreparable as you thought. Two, taking the hyperbole out of failure will deflate its power as an excuse not to try. So that's exactly what we're about to do.

Start by painting a very detailed picture. Run the numbers. Do everything you can to quantify just how bad failure would be. Then look at your life beyond the job and estimate the impact. When you finish that whole exercise in oblivion, do one more thing: step up and acknowledge that, even though you've painted a picture that is far from pretty, you are still the same highly capable person and very little (barring the fallout of outright illegality or reckless stupidity) is not rebuildable. Now, quantify that! No really. Imagine you failed miserably and then plot a course back to where you were when you took the original risk. Not so hard is it?

When you are all done painting this picture, set it aside. Know that, whether it is your intention or not, every time you revisit this scenario you give it power. So, dive in to it in detail, wallow in it briefly if you really need to, then *let it go!*

Explore and Quantify Inaction—ONCE

Almost everyone thinks about the first question: What if I fail? In fact, they explore it often to the complete exclusion of two far more important, mobilizing questions: What if I don't even try? What if I succeed?

So, move on to the second one: What if I don't even try? What if I just keep on keeping on?

Play that out for a few years. Now for a few decades. Extrapolate the impact of continuing in your same career on your body, mind, and spirit. Examine its impact on your levels of life-sapping chronic stress and the effect that relentless stress, dissatisfaction, and disillusionment will have on your risk for diabetes, heart attack, stroke, cancer, anxiety, and depression.

Project what your body will look and feel like and write down how your emotional state will fare after years or decades down the same path you're traveling today. Imagine how all this will affect your relationships with your partner, kids, friends, and family.

If you think you are unfulfilled, unhealthy, and unhappy now, *do you really think those states will just hover at the same level after years or decades of the same?* Not a chance.

Nothing is innocuous. Not even your decision to avoid making a decision. So, if failure is largely recoverable and staying the course would create a depressing future, how could you justify *not* giving it a shot?

If you want to be fearful, go ahead, be afraid, but not of failure. Instead, be afraid of never trying, because that is the closest thing you have to a guaranteed downhill slide for the rest of your working life.

So, create your inaction visualization, digest it, then *let it go.*

Simulate Success—*DAILY*

Without clarity and belief, there is no action. If you don't know what to do or where you are going, you won't know what actions to take. If you know where you want to go, but don't believe you can get there, you won't act. And, without action, there is no accomplishment.

Clarity allows you to create vivid mental simulations. Repeating those simulations leads to belief. And belief fuels action.

Repeatedly visualizing a deeply sought-after goal, seeing, feeling, hearing yourself accomplish this goal, over and over, has a profound effect. It conditions you slowly away from self-doubt and disbelief and moves you increasingly toward belief.

And, when you believe something, even marginally, you begin to do a thousand little things differently. You talk to people you'd normally avoid. You ask questions you'd have been too shy to ask. You help people you'd normally ignore. You dress a little better. You interact with more confidence. You carry yourself differently.

You invest time, energy, hours, and funds in yourself and others without really noticing how differently you are presenting yourself to the world. To those who come in contact with you, you are different.

And the net result of those dozens of microscopic changes in your behavior, on a daily basis is twofold:

- People perceive you differently. They become responsive because they read in you a sense of confidence, commitment, and raw-energy that they want to participate in.
- All the little actions begin to add up. The thousands of nearly imperceptible changes in behavior and modest actions taken on a consistent, daily basis, begin to yield results that take you a step closer to your visualized goal.

Is It Better to Visualize the Goal or Visualize the Steps?

The approach to visualization or mental simulation most often offered is something called *outcome* simulation. It asks you to create a vivid picture of a specific outcome, as if it has already happened. Maybe it's crossing the finish line at a race, owning your dream house, toppling a government, getting an A on an exam, or doing your dream job for a living. Outcome simulation can be an effective tool. But, for many people, especially when it comes to the early days of a career revolution, outcome is not the most powerful tool in the visualization arsenal.

Indeed, there is a different approach to visualization that has been shown in a number of published studies to be significantly more powerful. It's called *process* simulation and, true to its name, it focuses on visualizing not the outcome or goal, but the steps and actions needed to get there.

In 1998, researchers divided eighty-four college students into three groups. Over a one-week period, for five minutes each day, students in the *process* simulation group visualized the actions and steps needed to complete a specified project. At the same time, students in the *outcome* simulation group visualized themselves having successfully completed the project. Students in a third control group did neither. The results were eye-opening.

- Compared to the control group, students in both the process and the outcome groups were more likely to begin the project on time. So, both process and outcome simulation got people acting earlier than no simulation.
- The students who visualized themselves having successfully completed the project were significantly more likely to complete it on time.
- The students who visualized the *steps* needed to complete the project, though, were more likely than both other groups to finish on time and they gener-

ally considered the assignment easier than students in the other groups.*

In a series of additional studies on undergraduate students in 1997 and 1999, students who engaged in daily process simulation in anticipation of an exam started studying earlier than those who simply visualized getting an A. With more study, not surprisingly, the process simulation group scored an average of eight points better on the exam than the outcome simulation group, who simply visualized getting an A.

How do we apply this knowledge to your career renegade journey? Every career renegade journey unfolds in two phases.

The beginning phase involves quite a bit of research, information gathering, and planning. It's the research and development or R&D phase. The R&D phase prepares you for the second, more-active phase, aggressive pursuit of a specific career goal.

During the R&D phase, it is nearly impossible to create an effective outcome simulation, *because you don't yet know where you are going.*

---

*S. E. Taylor, L. B. Pham, L. D. Rivkin, and D. A. Armor (1998). "Harnessing the Imagination: Mental Simulation, Self-regulation, and Coping." *American Psychologist* 53: 429–39.

This is where process visualization can really shine, because your driving force is to act daily in an effort to gather the information needed to establish and go after an ultimate goal. Process simulation fuels these daily actions. It drives you to carry out these daily steps and makes you more likely to start earlier, be more consistent, and experience these tasks as being less work.

At the beginning of each week in your R&D phase, write out a list of three to five daily actions that will help take you closer to your ultimate career renegade goal. At this point, many of these actions will be about getting enough information to figure out and test whether that goal is feasible. Write these actions down, then, every day, for five minutes, find a quiet place, sit or lie down, and visualize yourself with as much clarity as possible taking those steps and engaging in those actions.

Once you have gathered enough information and established enough knowledge to know, with a great degree of clarity, exactly what you'd like to accomplish, and done the research to be confident that its attainment is possible, then it's time to add outcome simulation to your daily renegade mind-set practices. Outcome visualization comes in many forms. You can create a visualization or vision board, attaching images that represent what your career and life will look and feel like once you've achieved your goal. You can write a vivid description or record the description as an audio file. Whatever expression you choose, don't replace your process simulation with outcome simulation, do them both every day.

This daily dual simulation will go a long way toward cultivating the mind-set needed to believe in your ability to pull off your career evolution and then take the actions needed to make it happen. Especially when added to the daily mind-set practices you'll discover a bit later in this book.

And, as a special reader-only resource, you can download prerecorded process and outcome simulations as MP3 audio files for free at CareerRenegade.com. Click on the "Reader's Vault" tab.

EIGHTEEN

How to Be a Renegade without Ending Up Divorced and Penniless

MY WIFE'S GRANDPA ALLEN AND Grandma Dotty were amazing people. At nearly ninety years old, they lived independently in the middle of New York City and refused to take cabs anywhere. They would walk or take buses all over the city. They'd survived the Great Depression, many wars, and had a unique sensibility about life. Grandpa Allen worked, for some forty years as a salesman for mega department store Gimbels, Macy's then-famed rival. That's the way it used to be. You'd get a job and do it for life. You were loyal to them and they to you.

My wife and I used to giggle about the fact that, for years, nearly every time we'd visit, one of the first things

Grandpa Allen would ask was, "So, do you think you'll be going back to the law soon?" Having retired on the pension he was promised decades earlier, what I was doing just didn't register with him. And, I was confident that after ninety years of living and thinking the way he was used to, it never would. So I never spent much time trying to show him how dramatically the career landscape had changed over the last thirty years. We never spoke about the rampant decay of loyalty in both directions, the collapse of the pension-model, or the fairly recent awakening to the profound effects of *not* doing what you loved for the vast majority of your life. I just didn't feel the need to go there.

But, when it came to my parents, my sister, my wife, and my closest friends, I did. I needed them to understand. I needed, at best, their absolute support and, at worst, their forbearance and patience.

It has become standard in self-help books these days to recommend that you shed those around you who criticize or try to bring you down from your dream. "You've got to extract negativity from your life," they say. Sorry, but I can't agree with this as a universal principle.

It is critically important to learn to identify those who offer constructive, honest feedback, who act out of genuine, heartfelt concern over the impact of your choices upon you and, if they're close enough, upon them. These are the people who will be with you for life, who are genuinely and deeply concerned for your future and well-being and the security of you and your family. You may have to cut some toxic, chronic naysayers out of your life, but there are certain key people you need to spend time convincing to get on board with the renegade mind-set.

These are folks to whom you can't simply say, "Just watch me!" You need to do everything you can to ensure they're with you for the transition—and then for life. Being told to lose them if they're not immediately willing to jump on the radical-departure train along with you isn't realistic. It sets up a nearly insurmountable roadblock to your journey to meaningful work and wealth. There's another way. You need to make them part of the team; I call them your inner circle.

Usually when you tell your loved ones you're going renegade, two major concerns arise. You'll need to spend a lot of energy and time preparing to address them if you want any hope of rallying those who you'll need most to your cause:

Are you going nuts or just waking up to something powerful and real? ·

What about the security and lifestyle of our family?

Navigating these concerns is not the easiest part of your path, but you'll need to answer them now, or suffer later.

Are You Going Nuts or Just Waking Up to Something Powerful and Real?

Frankly, most of your family and friends would rather hear you're just going nuts. Because there's a pretty well-defined response to mental disease: therapy, medication, or meditation (and possibly even all three). We may not know what works best, but at least we have some precedent for what to try. Once your crisis is being effectively managed, the family should be able to get back to business.

Actually, counseling isn't a bad idea. After years of a life-sucking career that often leaves you increasingly estranged from those who mean the most to you, feeling stressed-out, sleep deprived, unfit, angry, and just plain burned, you may, in fact, have joined the other 28 million Americans who are clinically depressed and the other 53 million Americans who suffer anxiety or panic disorders. These are very real, often increasingly disabling challenges. Adding meaning to your career may help ameliorate these feelings over time, but this book can't tell you what is most appropriate for you. You need a qualified mental-health professional to go all the way.

Also, this is going to be an incredible process, but it is also one loaded with surprises and emotion. Some people can manage that process themselves, but chances are it will be much more constructive and efficient with someone else, someone more skilled and objective than you serving as your guide and, sometimes, mediator between you and those who love you but disagree with what you are trying to achieve.

Besides, getting therapy will help show those who care about you and whose lives will be most directly touched by your actions that you are taking your exploration seriously and that you are looking to create the most intelligent, informed choice possible as you move forward. This goes a long way toward opening their ears and hearts when you begin to share what is on your mind.

Two other key factors are the proof and the plan. Part of your ability to win your family's support lies in your ability to show them that what you want to do is possible, that others have succeeded at it, and you have an intelligent plan to get you there.

If you're starting to get the feeling that you'll need to do a fair amount of work before you go public, you're right. I've thrown a lot of ideas up against the wall and have probably gone public with my desire to explore them a bit too early. When you do that you risk having your friends and family question whether they should stand behind you. I've learned, very much the hard way, to explore the viability of my nonstop stream of ideas a bit more fully before going public to that primary ring of support.

Prepare the Pitch

When rallying your inner circle, you'll want to approach the process like you're pitching for your life. You are. You might want to explore using a modified version of marketing legend Dan Kennedy's three-step sales process: "problem—agitate—anticipate/solve." Here's how it might work:

1. *Problem.* Identify the problem. For you, it will be some variation of "my current job is making me anxious, depressed, unfit, physically ill, dissociating me from my partner, kids, family, and good friends; and the trickle-down effect on the entire family is no longer worth the financial benefits."

2. *Agitate.* Point to research and examples. Go to CareerRenegade.com and download my report called "Breaking Research on the Connection Between Work, Wealth, and Happiness." This will arm you with a wealth of research on the very real impact of working in a career that empties your soul. Then, create a list of actual examples from your life that demonstrates, in a clear, incontrovertible way, how your specific career has negatively affected you, your relationships, and your family.

3. *Solve.* Present your solution. This is where you reveal your plan of action, explain how it solves the problem presented, and ask for support. But if you have someone very close to you who you believe, in your heart, will be capable of remaining open-minded and help you develop your plan, share what you are contemplating with that person. If not, before going public, you may want to have completed the information-gathering R&D phase (more on that below). Doing so will allow you to present a far more compelling, better thought out, more easily saleable, and defensible plan of action and solution.

4. *Anticipate and respond to objections.* One of the hallmarks of great salespeople is their ability to anticipate and respond to the major objections to any sale. This is, in large part, what we've done in this chapter. Your job, now, is to personalize the objections and overcome them by first validating and addressing each.

What About the Security and Lifestyle of Our Family?

I hate to break it to you, but no matter how rich you are, there is no such thing as financial security. One illness, lawsuit, or bad business decision and what took decades to accumulate can be wiped out in days. In fact, many hugely successful entrepreneurs have made and lost their fortunes multiple times. The element that allowed them to bounce back is also the closest anyone can come to true financial security: extreme competence.

Just because you're planning to leave the setting and career that has supported you to date doesn't mean you're also leaving your skills and proven ability to succeed. They go with you. You have a massive fallback in the guise of your own extraordinary competence. You've got a safety net, one that can go a long way toward getting your inner circle more comfortable with your decision to take your shot at a more meaningful working future.

When I left the law, I sat down with various members of my family and close friends and explained what I was about to do and why. I also reminded them that I was still a member of the bar, that I would maintain my license to practice, and, worst case, could always go back and pick up where I left off. Was that a desirable option for me? Of course not. In fact, not wanting to do just that became a strong motivator for me to succeed at something else. But for those who relied upon me for some sense of security and stability, it was a conversation that went a long way toward garnering the support or, at least, keeping extreme lack of support at bay long enough to show what I was capable of away from the law.

Show your inner circle how your competence goes with you, show them how you have an intelligent fallback, and how you will work incredibly hard to create a plan that includes the opportunity to not only get you back to where you were, but vault you past that same place. If need be, you might even consider negotiating a period of forbearance—get them to give you a certain number of months or years to make it work and then agree to return to something more mainstream should you fail within that time frame.

Show them, again, that this is deeply meaningful to you and they'll be part of the entire process. A process that leads to the final question you'll need to be ready to answer.

But, What About Our Lifestyle?

This is it. The biggie. The hurdle of all hurdles for those with families and substantial financial responsibilities. The answer everyone will be looking for is, "It won't, I guarantee it. If anything, we'll be better off." And you may in fact be. But, at least in the short term, depending on your desired path and your plan, you might not. So how do you handle this?

You may take a very real short-term hit to your earning ability, depending on your path. Maybe not. But it is critical to know and to share the understanding that, if planned for properly, a potential short-term dip in income need not necessarily translate to a hit to your standard of living during that same period of time.

When I was preparing to leave the law, I knew I was going into a field where most people made a fairly modest living. I believed that applying my business skills to a field where those skills were all too often sorely lacking should put me in a good place to significantly outperform the market. But I also knew I'd need to pay my dues for a short time to learn the market on a more realistic level than I could get from books, conversations, and interviews.

Ten months before I finally left the law, I began to plan. I didn't quite know what I would transition to or how it would work, but I knew I needed to leave and I had a strong notion that with my interests I'd make way too little to live on for the first six months to a year. So, as I continued to learn and plan, I also began to save. I cut back on luxury buys. I still lived, just a bit more modestly.

And, while I missed some of the niceties, I was surprisingly at peace with the knowledge that I was giving them up in the name of eventually pursuing a decades-long career that filled me up and delivered me back into a similar standard of living, but with a markedly improved quality of life.

Some of you will be able to retool what you do, while

staying where you are. Others will change positions while, again, staying in the same setting or company. The more successful you are, the more valuable you become to your employer and you may find them unexpectedly open to moving you into or creating a path within the same company that keeps you in their employ.

If you work for yourself, it may be a matter of changing the way you approach what you do, rather than completely abandoning it.

For those who are drawn to something radically different than what they are doing today, something that would require a more disruptive change, planning, saving, and learning are not the only options. Testing and building your next adventure gradually, on the side, is yet another option. Indeed, for many, it is the best option.

For those who think they don't have the time or energy to live a short-term double life, you'll be amazed at how those two precious resources seem to appear out of thin air when you're doing something that makes your heart flutter.

For many with stronger pedigrees and easier access to funds than I had when I left the law, there is a wide array of other transition strategies, including outside investment or leverage/debt that would allow you to maintain a nearly identical standard of living, while growing a happier and hopefully even more lucrative future, on someone else's dime.

When you sit down with your family and friends, show them that you've thought this through—that you have a plan in place—it will make a huge difference in their reaction. And who knows, you might even find your first employee among them!

NINETEEN

Don't Do It Alone

WE'VE ALREADY EXPLORED HOW TO cultivate support among your close friends and family, but, beyond the challenge of surviving negativity and building a base of support among your family and friends, there is a giant additional step you need to take to help ensure your successful pursuit of a lucrative and deeply meaningful career. You need to look to people who've already been where you're looking to go.

Who are these folks? That depends on what you're trying to accomplish. If you're lucky, they will teach you, guide you, accelerate your path to success, and inspire you by example. They are living proof that what you want to do is in fact possible. They are the ones who can draw from their own mold-breaking experiences to help you conceive of solutions you never dreamed of.

In *Vital Friends,* author Tom Rath identifies eight distinct roles of friends: builders, companions, connectors, collaborators, energizers, mind openers, navigators, and champions. Seek these people out wherever and whenever you can. They will become your inspiration, your catalysts, your collaborators, and accelerators. They will keep you focused not on what needs to be surmounted, but on what is possible, no matter how fierce the challenge becomes. Your first challenge is getting in touch with them and convincing them to be part of your journey.

Start with personal contacts. Put the word out among your personal contacts that you are interested in connecting with people who have done X. Start with your close connections, but do *not* skip over your loose or casual connections.

According to a study published in the *American Journal of Sociology* that looked at people who found new jobs through connections, 16.7 percent relied upon close connections (people they saw weekly), while 27.8 percent found new jobs through connections they rarely ever saw (less than once a year). So when prospecting for potential members of your upper circle (sources of inspiration, constructive feedback, and direction) look a bit deeper into your

Rolodex than who you've lunched with or spoken to in the last month.

Then, take action. Allow your connections to bridge the gap, providing an introduction. Reach out to your contacts and say something like, "I am researching a shift in career to do _____ and would really love to speak with anyone who's already in this field to get more information. I wonder if you might know anyone and, if so, would you be kind enough to help me with an introduction." An introduction always works best, but even without one, you can still call, e-mail, stop by, whatever is most appropriate for the person you'd like to meet. You may be surprised by how many people you find.

Take your search online. Search for individuals in areas of interest who, again, have accomplished some or all of what you are looking to do. If they are reachable, then reach out to them directly by e-mail or telephone.

These people will become your upper circle. They are your team and the more time and effort you invest in them, the more powerful you will become together.

Remember one thing too, the more well-known a person is, the less time and energy they will likely have for you, even if you get their attention. So while it would be cool to have Virgin's Richard Branson (Richard, call me), former General Electric CEO Jack Welch, or *Blink* author

Malcolm Gladwell on your team, you'll very likely be better served by an upper circle with the time and incentive to learn more about you and take a more active role in guiding and mentoring your decisions. Pursue knowledge and involvement, not fame.

If you still want to go for higher-profile people, here are some additional ways to get their attention and, potentially, a few minutes of their time.

Send an e-mail: This sounds so easy, most people just assume it would never work. But I have to tell you, if you reach out directly to someone in a respectful way, you'd be surprised how many people will respond.

Marketing guru and *New York Times* bestselling author Seth Godin has been someone I've admired for some time. A few months into blogging, I was working on a roundup article on marketing and I thought it would be incredibly cool to have Seth's insights. My first instinct was to just assume he'd be too busy. After all, I was a newbie blogger with barely a hint of an online reputation.

But, then I figured, "Why not try?" So, I sent him a quick e-mail and, within minutes, he replied with some great information.

Will this always work? No. Most of the time, it won't. But, it costs you nothing to try, so why not give it a shot?

Tips for E-mailing Higher-Profile People

In the subject, write something like, "Quick question about [insert highly relevant topic]." Use the subject-line to pique interest, not trick.

Be brief and to the point

Tell them, in a single sentence, why you are e-mailing

Ask your question

Thank them

Provide multiple modes of contact in your signature file, this allows them to reply in the mode that is most natural to them. This is a lesson I learned writing this book. Some people prefer e-mail, others phone, others want to sit with you, so give the recipient enough information to choose their preferred mode of reply.

Send something relevant and cool: Take the PR approach with a modern slant. Research the person, read everything you can find about them online and offline. Find out what their business and personal interests are, then overnight them an inexpensive token that shows you've invested in learning who they are and include a note that says something like, "You've been an incredible inspiration to me on a business level. I particularly enjoyed your recent [insert your comment on blog post/news story/Twitter excerpt/accomplishment]. I am curious about [fill in a single question you would like answered] and wonder if you might share your thoughts at some point in the manner that's most convenient to you. You can reach me at: insert your e-mail/Twitter/mail]."

Why use overnight mail? Two reasons. One, an overnight package stands out more than an envelope on someone's desk. Two, because overnight delivery is much more costly than mail, it tells the recipient you are likely not mass mailing people a similar request. This lends credibility to your claim that you have sought them out for their individual expertise.

Will they reply? Maybe, maybe not. Most won't, but some will. And what's the harm in trying?

When I launched Sonic Yoga, I had miniature yoga bags made and put our press materials in them, rolled up like yoga mats. I then researched the top health and lifestyle editors in New York, found out who covered yoga and had the bags hand delivered with personal notes attached. Within hours, the phone started ringing off the hook. Even editors who never wrote about us still called just to say hello and share how cool the bags were. Some even asked us to send slightly bigger ones for water bottles. While this example is grounded in PR, not mentoring, it's simply an example of getting the attention and response of people who are generally considered nearly impossible to reach.

Two major caveats. One, do *not* stalk anyone. If you do not get a reply, try once more with a different enclosure a month or two later, then let it rest. Two, do not use people's home addresses. These days, you can find nearly anyone's home contact information online. Don't use it. Even though reaching out to someone at home may cut through layers of screening, many people will view this as a violation of their personal boundaries and be strongly put off by it.

Find out if they blog, micro-blog (e.g., Twitter), or participate in any online forums: More and more, top-tier professionals, authors, professors, and entrepreneurs blog, micro-blog, or participate in online forums. Some do it as a way to share what's on their minds, others do it in a concerted effort to create channels of communication with customers, colleagues, and the huddled masses. Either way, read, friend, and follow them online, especially if you can find them hanging out in more leading-edge forums, like micro-blogging or lifestreaming, where the conversation tends to be more open and casual.

If you consistently read and listen to what these folks have to say, offer thoughtful, genuine, and valuable comments and conversation, over time, you'll become a bit of a known entity to them. It's the marketing equivalent of warming your audience, so when you finally reach out to make the sale or, in your case, ask for a few minutes of their time, they'll be more receptive.

One more thing, the more you can establish your profile online as someone who adds value to conversations, the more likely you'll be to get the ears, eyes, and keyboards of higher-profile web communicators.

Join an organization that your upper-circle prospects belong to: Volunteer to participate actively. Even if this does not expose you directly to the person you want to connect with, over time you will become a known entity both within the organization and to those who have the ear of individuals you'd like to connect with. When you finally reach out, your audience will have been primed and you will be more likely to get through.

A word of caution, though, with all of these access techniques—make sure you have a *genuine interest* in the individual or organization and their mission before reaching out to someone or joining a group. Seek to connect and participate because you care about what that person has to offer or are invested in a group's mission and are willing to contribute to that mission, even if it never leads to the desired connection. Fakery never bodes for a fruitful experience.

The more people you can rally to not only support, but advise you on your journey, the greater your likelihood of success. Start with your friends and family, then expand outward until the team you need is solidly in place. You may need to make a lot of calls, send a lot of e-mails, and have a lot of coffee dates, but in the end, it will be worth the effort.

What If You Want to Do Something That's Never Been Done Before?

The greatest challenge in this arena will be for those of you whose journey involves not just thinking outside the box, but literally building a box that doesn't yet exist.

How can you find a mentor who's already done what you want to do when nobody's ever done what you want to do? The answer is not nearly as complicated as you might think.

Sure, the content and method of what you are about to do may never have been done before. When Steve Jobs set out to create a computer capable of sitting on the desktop of every home, he didn't have a lead to follow in the world of desktop computers. However, I've found that there is tremendous crossover in the approach, methodology, lessons, and inspiration that drives the vast majority of product or paradigm-creating innovators in any field. Real innovators usually have:

- A deep passion for the content, beyond the desire to make money.
- A clear picture of the gap in the market of the problem in need of a solution.
- A nearly unshakable commitment to solving a problem or doing something better than it's been done before.
- A willingness to take risks and make decisions based on the best information available relatively quickly, even if it's not all of the information that might be accessible over a longer period of time. Entrepreneurs refer to this as the ready-fire-aim mind-set.
- An ability to visualize a solution that does not exist or at least to see the possibility of the solution.

The people who have manifested these qualities and succeeded in creating solutions, businesses, products, or services that simply did not exist before are the ones you need to seek out.

TWENTY

Hold On to Your Life Preserver Until You Can Swim

VERY OFTEN, THE MORE ENTRENCHED you are in your current path, the harder it is to convince yourself that you'll be okay doing something else. Some changes call for short, dramatic transitions, while others allow for the gradual build up of expertise, assets, and confidence needed to make the jump.

Leo's Story
Father of Six Finds Opportunity Online

Remember Guam-based father of six, journalist and speechwriter, Leo Babauta? As a sports writer, editor, and journalist for Guam's largest newspaper, Leo's career was extremely demanding and the hours were maddening. But, with six kids and a wife to support, Leo didn't have the option to take time off or retrain for a different profession. So, he repurposed his skills and took a job with more normal hours as a speechwriter, while picking up freelance work on the side.

The more humane schedule helped Leo balance his life, but he still hoped to find more meaningful work. How he did this, though, surprised even him.

Leo had been through a lot of struggle in his life and overcame many obstacles and wanted to share the benefit of his experiences. As we've seen a number of people do, he began to blog.

In early 2007, Leo launched ZenHabits.net and, drawing upon decades of experience as a journalist, began to write powerful articles every day and share them online. At first, just his family and a few friends read Leo's blog. But soon enough others began to discover the blog. And, a few months in, driven largely by Leo's humility, willingness to share his journey, and ability to write, ZenHabits.net began to pick up steam.

Seeing an opportunity to redeploy his skills, sharing his stories and burgeoning passion for productivity and simplicity to create a new source of income, Leo dove headlong into a double life, working as a speechwriter and journalist by day and a productivity and life-advice guru by night. Within months, his authentic voice and mission-driven effort led to explosive growth in readership and ad-driven revenue.

Six months into blogging, the income generated by ZenHabits.net almost matched that of Leo's day jobs. But he was essentially now working two jobs and, with six kids and a wife he loved to spend time with, the pace was tough. So, he began to brainstorm ways to accelerate his move away from his seventeen-year career in print journalism.

Leo assembled his thoughts into a productivity e-book called Zen to Done and then released it online, using his blog and growing network of virtual friends to get the word out. It was then priced at about $20. The e-book sold over one thousand copies in a matter of weeks.

This brought Leo's dream of finally earning a living writing about what he loved even closer and it opened up an even bigger opportunity, a book deal with a major publisher. Leo was in heaven. A year into his double life as a blogger, e-book author, speechwriter, and journalist, on January 23, 2008, Leo proudly announced to the world,

> Today is that day. I'm living my dream. Of course, I always thought I'd do it writing fiction, but still . . . the thought of seeing my name on the cover of a book . . . it's still unbelievable to me. I don't think I'll really believe it until I see it. The book deal has also helped me realize my dream of being a full-time blogger (and writer), giving me that extra financial security needed to quit my day job.

With his kids and wife in tow, Leo's yearlong double life had delivered on the promise of a full-time career doing what he loved.

In Leo's case, his double life was fueled by the need to grow his passion-driven career into a substantial enough source of income to be able to support his family.

For Dr. Joe Alban, though, his twenty-year evolution was more about convincing himself his new career would satisfy his desire to improve peoples' lives, and also get comfortable with the notion of leaving a career that took decades of formal education and practice to master. Joe's story is an amazing testament to the blended power of passion and patience.

=== *Joe's Story*
Doc Finds Solace in Coffee

During his last year of surgical residency in Chicago, Dr. Joe Alban did a two-week stint as a cruise doctor in Hawaii for the American Hawaii Cruise Ships. While in the islands, he fell in love with a girl named Deepa, an island named Kona, and coffee that warmed the soul. But, his future was in medicine, not Kona and coffee.

Finishing his residency six months later, Joe moved back to Orange County, California, to start his practice. Soon after, Deepa moved to California to be with him and about a year later they got married.

Life as a surgeon was tough, but Joe loved helping people. He and Deepa dreamed of retiring to Kona, so they bought a little piece of land there and vacationed there as often as possible, making friends and even planting coffee trees, so Joe would have something to do when he retired.

As the trees began to mature, Deepa began to market the little bit of coffee they were growing. I don't know what the Hawaiian word for cojones is, but it sounds like Deepa had them. Rather than start small, she immediately thought big. She hopped on a plane to Dallas to call on buyers from her favorite store, Neiman Marcus . . . and landed the account. With that, Kona Joe Coffee was officially in business.

Joe began to spend more time on Kona playing with ways to grow a better coffee bean.

Joe and Deepa were having a ball in their new coffee adventure, but, while Deepa stayed on the island increasingly, Joe was still living a double life. Dr. Joe by day and the caped coffee crusader by night.

As Kona Joe Coffee grew, Joe realized something extraordinary. "There was a satisfaction that I was getting from making something that many, many people could enjoy," he shared, "without the stress of emergencies in the middle of the night, or possible loss of life or limb, that I could get some of that same satisfaction of making people's lives better, but doing something that's a lot more fun and relaxing for myself."

Joe began to realize growing and sharing his coffee had become an alternate career path. To take Kona Joe Coffee to the next level, though, they would need to invest much more heavily in buildings and equipment. It was nearly twenty years into his double life as a surgeon and coffee grower that Joe took a massive leap of faith. In 2003, he sold the house in Orange County and used the money to take their coffee dream to a whole new level. Joe kept commuting every two weeks, but quickly grew tired of living out of the local Residence Inn for two weeks at a time and flying home to Kona.

Finally, in 2004, Joe made the break, leaving his medical career behind at the age of forty-seven and turning to an adventure he'd only *dreamed of for decades. Interestingly enough, he says he probably sees his friends more now than he ever did as a doctor. Everyone wants to visit, the weather is always gorgeous, and because his friends are always on vacation when they come to visit, they're always in great moods, making their time together that much more enjoyable.*

Joe's quality of life is dramatically improved. He lives in paradise, spends most of his time outside doing things he loves to do with people he loves to be around. "I really just look forward to each day," says Joe, "you know, to the interesting people we're going to meet or the visitors coming to the farm for tours and other people in the coffee industry who come from all over the world . . . it's opened up our lives to meeting a breadth of humanity that I would never have had exposure to as a doctor."

I was surprised to learn, too, that the long-term economic potential of Kona Joe Coffee will likely far exceed what he could've ever made as a surgeon.

Joe's story speaks to the patience involved in seeing the next step even if it's years or decades off and committing to an incremental process of reeducation and building that fits within your lifestyle. For some, gratification can come quickly, for others, the far more intelligent path is a slow build.

But . . . Understand the Limits of Toe Dipping

Dr. Joe spent a lot of time easing his way from Dr. Joe to Kona Joe and had the support of an incredible life partner and, eventually, business partner. One thing that became clear to most people who lived split lives, though, was that the next leg of the journey could never really take off the way it needed to until the decision to fully commit to it was made.

Nor, for that matter, will you ever be able to judge the viability of that second career until you make it your priority. Very often, it's that final, excruciatingly small bit of energy that pushes an idea from treading water to all-out success.

TWENTY-ONE

Be Your Own Guru

Do not go where the path may lead; go instead where there
is no path and leave a trail.

—RALPH WALDO EMERSON

I SPENT THE BETTER PART of the first forty years
of my life looking for a guru, a person who would just blow
me away with her or his prescience, kindness, compassion,
vision, and guidance. The one who would give me the an
swers. Who would tell me what to do to get to that place
where I finally felt like I had "made it."

So many others I knew had found a guru and their lives
seemed so much better, more directed and purposeful for it,
but that never happened to me.

I would attend lectures, teachings, seminars, trainings,
and retreats and inevitably end up leaving early because

some combination of information, integrity, pace, or delivery did not resonate. Why couldn't I find that person?

It finally dawned upon me: The person I was looking for was the one I would need to become.

Others can offer guidance. They can share what they know from their own lives or the teachings of their teachers. Classical texts like the Bhagavad Gita, the Bible, the Talmud, the Koran, and the occasional Bazooka Joe comic lend intelligence to the process of discovery.

But, in the end, no one else can stand in my shoes. No one else can live my fears, dreams, loves, relationships, desires, intellect, challenges, life, and lifestyle. No one else can enjoy or suffer the outcome of my decisions or actions. No one else is better equipped to know me. No one else can take action but me.

Upon that realization, I began to accept responsibility not only for my life to date, but for the process of making it come alive from that point forward. Not for anyone else. For me.

I continued to listen to conventional wisdom, but, realizing most who followed it ended up not more, but less fulfilled, I committed to forming my decisions another way. I adopted a standard that guides nearly every major business decision I make. The standard of the career renegade.

"Will this career choice," I ask, "let me spend the greatest amount of time absorbed in activities and relationships that make me come alive, while earning the living I need to live?"

When I started making decisions from this place, the world seemed to increasingly become my partner in the career adventure of a lifetime. Does that mean everything started to come easily? No.

In case you haven't gathered from this book, creating your life and livelihood to deliver maximum passion and prosperity is a gargantuan challenge. But, it's one worth engaging in. And, recent advances in technology have made possible options and opportunities that simply did not exist even a few short years ago.

I can't tell you where or how it's going to end. And frankly, taking full responsibility for the state of my life and happiness still scares the hell out of me on a pretty regular basis. But far less than it would scare me to turn it over to someone else and simply hope for the best.

I cannot conduct the balance of my life in a vacuum of inevitable regret. I cannot imagine the sorrow of leaving this Earth one day filled with visions of a life I dreamed of living, but never had the will to try. I cannot rest with the notion that, in my inaction, I might have taught my daughter to do the same.

Like Helen Keller said, "Life is either a daring adventure, or nothing."

What are you waiting for?

Appendix

CAREER RENEGADE PROGRAMS

CareerRenegade.com Website and Blog.

Visit the Career Renegade website and blog on a regular basis for free daily-dispatches, articles, advice-columns, video case-studies, tools, techniques, and event schedule updates.

Career Renegade Live Trainings, Mentoring Circle, and Events.

Are you looking for more hands-on guidance? I will be offering a number of different live trainings and events throughout the year, from a few hours to a few days long and admitting a limited number of people to my private mentoring circle. Visit www.CareerRenegade.com for details.

Speaking Engagements.

In case you didn't gather from this book . . . I speak. Topics span entrepreneurship to marketing, writing to PR, and stress management to the critical importance of doing what you love, even if you're working for someone else. My guiding philosophy anytime I speak is to offer information that is insanely useful, highly engaging, and immediately actionable. I love to share stories, thoughts, and principles that make lightbulbs go on. But, as you also might have guessed, nothing is more important than family to me, so I don't do the national circuit thing and I keep my speaking schedule limited to a very select number of engagements in any given season. *To inquire about booking a speaking engagement, visit www.CareerRenegade.com or e-mail speaking @careerrenegade.com.*

Jonathan Fields.com.

In addition to the resources above, you can also find extensive marketing, copywriting, PR, small business, and lifestyle tips, tools, articles, and communities at my personal blog.

For additional information on any of these programs, visit www.CareerRenegade.com.

About the Author

Jonathan Fields, hedge-fund lawyer turned serial entrepreneur, speaker, marketer, and blogger, has been featured in the *New York Times, Business Week,* the *Wall Street Journal, CNBC, Entrepreneur, Fine Living, Today, Vogue, Self, Elle, Outside, Small Business Success,* and thousands of websites. He currently oversees his entrepreneurship-training company, Career Renegade, Inc., his interactive/direct-marketing group, Vibe Creative, and the Manhattan yoga center, Sonic Yoga. Jonathan also writes a widely read lifestyle blog at JonathanFields.com and contributes to many other top blogs and magazines. When not playing at work, he can be found dancing around his living room with his daughter and wife. Occasionally, he sleeps.